The Wild Red Deer of Killarney

THE WILD RED DEER OF KILLARNEY

*A Personal Experience
and Photographic Record
of the Yearly and Life Cycles
of the Native Irish Red Deer
of County Kerry*

Seán Ryan

First published in 1998 by
Mount Eagle Publications Ltd.,
Dingle, Co. Kerry, Ireland

Text and Photographs © Seán Ryan 1998

The author has asserted his moral rights.

ISBN 1 902011 09 0

The map on page 120 is based on Ordnance Survey Ireland
by permission of the Government Permit No 6738
© Government of Ireland

This publication has received support from the
Heritage Council under the 1998 Publications Grant Schemes

Typesetting by Red Barn Publishing, Skeagh, Skibbereen

Cover design by the Public Communications Centre, Dublin

Printed in Singapore

Contents

For Peggy, Patricia, Matt and Colm

Foreword

I first met Seán Ryan in the early 1980s, just before a talk on the wild red deer of Killarney that he gave to our student Zoological Society. The audience responded uniquely, with sustained applause, not only at the end, but also in the middle of the lecture. Seán had been describing the rut, and illustrated this with a series of breathtaking slides of stags on the mountainside roaring in defense of their hinds. These he backed with a tape-recording of the roars. The students were stunned; for a moment they felt themselves actually there; their applause was spontaneous. This book may have a similar effect on its readers.

Seán Ryan began his studies on the red deer of Killarney – the sole remnant of our native deer – in the early 1960s. The animals had long been regarded simply as a commercial resource, for deerstalking, and were then not far from extinction. Seán, an accountant living in Cork city, decided to obtain a photographic record of them before they vanished, an event which happily, due to a dawning realisation of their importance and to changing attitudes to wildlife generally, was averted. The photographic record became something of an obsession. Most weekends, and odd holidays, were spent on the Killarney mountains pursuing it, even in the depths of winter. But he also kept a journal of his observations with a care and attention to detail characteristic of his profession. He quizzed the staff of Killarney National Park on their experiences with the deer. He ferreted into the history of the herd and read widely on red deer in other parts of the world. Inevitably, he became an expert.

Books on Irish wildlife are far from plentiful, and even general ones, some of which are entirely superficial, are scarce. Authoritative volumes on particular groups of Irish animals, other than birds, are even rarer. To my knowledge, there has to date been no serious book on a single species of wild animal in Ireland, other than a bird or fish. *The Wild Red Deer of Killarney* is therefore a major event in Irish publishing, and is in the finest traditions of wildlife writing, with appeal to interested layman and professional naturalist alike. Even before beginning, the appetite of the reader will be whetted by the many fascinating colour photographs, the pick from innumerable rolls of film.

This book is an original. It describes the life of the beast, first-hand, as it really is, with traits both endearing and otherwise, in the often harsh environment of the Kerry mountains. It follows the animals through the year, from the relative peace and lush conditions of summer, into the sex and violence of the rut in autumn, through the bitter mountain winter, to spring when, before the fresh grazing of the year appears, death finally overtakes those aged and the weak that have survived.

James S. Fairley, DSc, PhD, MRIA
Associate Professor of Zoology, National University of Ireland, Galway

Acknowledgements

A very special and sincere thanks to Professor James S. Fairley, at the National University of Ireland, Galway, who many years ago first encouraged me to write this book, and who, as well as critically reading the manuscript and writing the foreword, has assisted its publication in many ways.

I also wish to thank Dr Paddy Sleeman and Dr Tom Kelly, both of the Zoology Department at the National University of Ireland, Cork, for listening patiently to many questions, and being always willing to provide literature and advice.

Thanks are also due to the staff of Killarney National Park, especially to Dan Kelleher, Park Superintendent, and to Dr Jim Larner, biologist, for their friendship and advice, which has always been freely given. I am greatly indebted to the Park Rangers - to head Ranger Paudie O'Leary; and to Rangers Tim Burkitt, Terry Carruthers, Paudie Cremin (now retired), Pascal Dower, John O'Connor, Brendan O'Shea, Padraig O'Sullivan and Peter O'Toole, for their continued friendship over the years, and good humour - even on wet days. A special thank you to Peter, for his kindness in waiting while one more photograph was being taken. Thanks to Mr Charles J Haughey for permission to visit Inishvicillaun and the hospitality provided, and to Senator Tom Fitzgerald and Tom O'Flaherty who made my stay there so memorable.

Thanks also to Elizabeth Drummond and Paula Heffernan, who typed the first drafts of the manuscript. And thanks to very many others, far too numerous to list individually, but who will know that I am greatly in their debt.

Last, but certainly by no means least, my deeply felt thanks to my wife Peggy and our family, for the great patience and faithful support I have always enjoyed.

I am most grateful to you all.

All opinions, expressed or implied, and all errors are solely mine.

Introduction

The earliest accurately dated record of red deer *Cervus elaphus* in Ireland goes back 26,000 years before the present (BP). There is another at 11,800 years BP, and further reliable records become more frequent from about 6,000 years BP. The earliest accurately dated record of red deer in Kerry, so far, is 4,000 years BP, at Ventry Beach.

Natural historians have repeatedly stated that red deer are indigenous to Ireland, meaning that they came here naturally, and were here before the earliest record of man (about 9,000 years BP). The three other native deer species whose remains have been found – the Giant Irish elk *Megaloceros giganteus*, the European elk *Alces alces*, and the reindeer *Rangifer tarandus* – are considered to have been extinct before man's arrival.

While red deer feature in the archaeological record, their remains are infrequent, and the evidence suggests that they were not an important food item for man, but that their antlers, bones and skins were used in the manufacture of tools, personal ornaments and clothing. There is no support in Irish archaeological findings for the romantic mass hunts and kills of red deer, as described in Gaelic myth and legend. In early Irish nature poetry, from about the ninth century onwards, the descriptive treatment of red deer leaves no doubt of personal observations of them, and of admiration for their beauty.

Fallow deer *Dama dama* were introduced into the country by the Normans in the twelfth century, to stock their deer parks. From then until the nineteenth century, just these two species – red and fallow – inhabited Ireland. Red deer were hunted with large deerhounds or rough-coated greyhounds, that pursued by sight, the huntsmen following on foot and horseback. Deer were also driven through narrow mountain passes and ambushed, or into specially prepared enclosures which narrowed into traps. Later, wild red deer and the emparked fallow were hunted by beagles – hounds that chased by scent – and followed by horsemen. From the late seventeenth century, and throughout the eighteenth century, the native red deer, together with such fallow deer as had escaped from parks and had run wild, were subjected to sustained slaughter, as part of a general exploitation of the country. This, together with the massive destruction of woodland and an increasing human population, resulted in the red deer, by the early nineteenth century, being reduced to scattered remnant populations, confined to the wild, remote and mountainous areas of the south-west, west and north-west.

The Great Famine of 1845–49 devastated the last traces of native red deer, as it did everything in Irish life. By the mid-nineteenth century they were reported as being still plentiful in Killarney, but only a few remained in the mountains of Connemara, Sligo, Donegal and Tipperary, and even the existence of some of these was by then only hearsay. The Great Famine and its aftermath saw all of these remnants perish, with the single exception of the Killarney red deer. These had been given protection by the two great landlords of Killarney, the Herberts of Muckross and the Brownes, Earls of Kenmare, both of whom established deer forests in the 1840s in the mountains around the Lakes of Killarney, for hunting and stalking purposes. Both deer forests – the Muckross forest and the Kenmare forest – marched side by side, sharing the same herds of red deer. The term "deer forest" has a special meaning: an area of unenclosed land, with or *without* woodland, set aside for the exclusive hunting and stalking of deer.

In Killarney, the stag hunt was a famous spectacle, put on for the amusement of the landed gentry of Killarney and for distinguished visitors. It was staged in most years from the eighteenth until the last quarter of the nineteenth century. It, too, was affected by the Famine and eventually ceased. It was replaced by the Scottish type of deer-stalking, where the individual stalker, accompanied by a gamekeeper and gillies, stealthily approached to within rifle shot of a selected stag.

In common with the accepted English and Scottish practice of introducing fresh blood to deer forests, in the belief that this would improve trophy heads of antlers – the basis on which the sport of deerstalking was built – five red stags were brought to Killarney from County Roscommon in the second half of the nineteenth century. At the end of the nineteenth and beginning of the twentieth centuries, some red deer from Killarney were sent to Scotland, and Scottish red deer were in turn imported to Killarney. The numbers involved are unknown.

Roe deer *Capreolus capreolus* had never been recorded in Irish archaeology, but were introduced in the nineteenth century to County Sligo. They were shot to extinction some decades later, because they damaged woodland. One other deer species was introduced, also in the nineteenth century, the Japanese sika *Cervus nippon*, to Powerscourt, County Wicklow, and this species has survived. From there it was brought to the woods of Muckross in 1865, as a game or sporting object, and was also extensively stalked in both the Muckross and Kenmare deer forests.

Reforms of land ownership, and the Land Acts of the late nineteenth and early twentieth centuries, spelled the end of the landed ascendancy. The Herbert and the Browne estates became heavily encumbered with debts, and were eventually sold. The Herbert estate of Muckross was purchased in 1899 by Lord Ardilaun, who leased it for stalking purposes, and then disposed of it in 1910 to William Bowers Bourn, an American millionaire. The estate was occupied by his daughter Maud and her husband, Arthur Rose Vincent, on whom the property was settled in 1916. In 1932 the entire Muckross estate, including the red deer herd and deer forest – in all about

4,300 hectares – was given as a gift to the Irish nation by William Bowers Bourn and Arthur Rose Vincent, to be called the Bourn-Vincent Memorial Park, in memory of Maud, who had died in 1929. It was Ireland's first national park. It has been administered since 1933 by the Office of Public Works (OPW), and since 1991 by the National Parks and Wildlife Service (NPWS). Throughout, deerstalking continued under the various owners, from the 1840s until 1964, when commercial deerstalking and shooting was abolished by the OPW.

The Kenmare estate continued in the ownership of the Earls of Kenmare, but much of it had been sold off by the early twentieth century. However, the deer forest remained intact, and deerstalking continued, as in the adjoining Muckross estate. In the 1970s parts of the Kenmare estate, including some of its deer forest, were purchased by the OPW. In 1985, following the death of Mrs Beatrice Grosvenor, the last family member who lived there, the remainder of the deer forest was acquired and incorporated with the Bourn-Vincent Memorial Park into today's Killarney National Park of 10,129 hectares. Deerstalking had finally ceased in the Kenmare estate by 1972, when all firearms above a specified calibre were prohibited under a special government order.

By 1994, numbers of red deer in the mountains of the Killarney National Park had increased from 110 in 1970, when accurate counts began, to 490. Reliable counts of deer in the lowlands have only been achieved in recent years. In 1994 there were 160, bringing the total to 690 in the park as a whole. Both the native reds and the introduced sika roam the same lowland and mountain habitats in the park. For a long time the herds of red deer which occupy mountain and lowland were considered to be discrete. Recent research has shown that the lowland herd can be considered as two groups, inhabiting Knockreer and Muckross respectively, with some interchange occurring between the Muckross group and the mountain herd.

Terminology

In Ireland, when a mountain man speaks of "going to the hill", he may mean anything from 200 to 1,000 metres. In the same tradition, "mountain" and "hill" are here used to mean the same thing.

It is customary today to apply the terms "stag" and "hind" to male and female sika deer, just in the way that they have always been used for red deer. But in Killarney this was never the custom until about the 1980s, when the copying of British stalking terminology became fashionable. Up until then the words always used in Killarney for sika male and female were "buck" and "doe", the same as those applied to fallow deer. "Buck" and "doe" appear throughout the literature on Killarney deer, and were the terms used by Lord Ardilaun, by A. R. Vincent and by the OPW when publicly advertising the deer shootings for letting in English sporting journals and in circulars to shooting agents and syndicates. These were also the language of local people in Killarney. When a hill man spoke of a buck or a stag, it was perfectly clear that he was referring to a either a sika or a red deer respectively. That older and distinctive terminology is retained in this book.

Other terms specific to deer are explained as they occur in the text.

The anglicisation of Irish placenames, which resulted in corrupt forms of the original Irish, is common in Killarney. Where possible, the phonetic usage of the word is retained in the text. Thus, for example, the mountain termed "Cromaglan" on Ordnance maps (part of the original Kenmare deer forest) would, in south Kerry where the emphasis is on the second or third syllable, be pronounced "Croma-GLOUN", and as "Cromagloun" it appears in the text. Placenames as used throughout are shown where possible on the accompanying map.

The adjective "indigenous", explained above, is properly applied to the Killarney red deer. However, in everyday usage the adjective "native" is taken to mean the same thing. Both are used in the text as being synonymous.

Important Warning

It is stressed that wild red stags cannot be trusted, especially during the rutting period. And the mountain environment is a harsh and unforgiving one; swift weather changes are normal, and can cause fatalities. The Kerry mountains are regularly underestimated and underrated. Since 1966, 35 people have been killed in them. Persons intending to venture into these mountains should be aware of the dangers inherent in all mountain terrain, and should seek advice from recognised mountaineering organisations.

I

Summer

Melldach rée rann:
  ro fáith gaíth garb gam;
gel ros; toirthech tonn;
  oll síd; subach sam.

Delightful the season: winter's harsh wind has departed; woodland is bright; water fruitful; peace is immense; summer is joyous.

Irish poem, 9th century [1]

Summer comes late to the mountains; frequently it is early June before full greening has pushed to the summits. Life now commences for the red deer calf. Most hinds that are pregnant are obviously so from about mid-May onwards. A pregnant hind is less active and lies about more than others. As the time for giving birth draws near, she withdraws from the rest of the herd and usually drives away her family group – daughters and sons of up to two years old.

The selection of the birth site is rarely witnessed because the hind has become so secretive. A calf can be born in a wide variety of terrain. Red deer occupy the entire range, from Killarney's lakeshores and woodland, at an altitude of less than 30 metres, to mountainside at 600 metres, where there is a preference for birth-sites between 300 and 500 metres. Most favoured are the high benches (broad level shelves) of Torc and the Cromagloun-Stompacoumeen and Poulagower-Knockrower ranges, and the Ferta slopes of Mangerton. Calves born at lower altitudes are frequently hidden in the tall fronds of fresh green bracken; those dropped on the slopes higher up are concealed amongst heather and grass tussocks, frequently near boulders and rock outcrops.

Before giving birth, a hind sometimes utters a calving bellow: a call that is evocative and somewhat mournful, which echoes amongst the hills and high coums. Immediately after calving, she licks her young one clean of the protective membrane which covers it at birth. This brings the coat to a glossy condition, preparing her calf for mountain weather. The licking also imprints the hind's own exclusive self – her smells and her voice – on the calf. From now on the calf knows its mother and the hind her own offspring, and will not confuse it with any other. The placenta (afterbirth) is cast and eaten by the hind. This has the obvious advantage of reducing the likelihood of the smell of blood attracting predators. Besides, the placenta is a rich source of nourishment and is not wasted by the hind, a particularly important point in a harsh mountain environment. Its consumption may also stimulate milkflow.

The birth of calves in the wild is very rarely witnessed or photographed. The illustration shows a hind galloping on the Ferta slopes, with a calf half born, its hooves and part of its front legs just emerging. The whole incident was quickly over. The hind had obviously been disturbed higher up and was now running downhill. She crossed broken ground with ease, between large boulders and through thick furze, with no obvious ill-effect. I watched her from a distance of about 800 metres and saw her emerge on to a grassy slope below, and walk normally, the calf's two front legs still protruding. When she reached a stream, she stopped and drank, then climbed the opposite bank and vanished into other rough ground.

Whether she was trying to cast a still-born calf, or whether the calf was subsequently born alive and healthy, is not known. However, if a hind could delay birth and gallop off, and put a safe distance between herself and a predator, this would be of benefit. Of course, no large predators roam the Kerry mountains today – the wolf disappeared over two hundred years ago[2] – but an inherent ability to avoid predation at the crucial time of birth may still remain. On a subsequent occasion, a park ranger witnessed a similar incident, which ended in a normal birth, and the calf was afterwards tagged[3].

Notwithstanding, difficult births do occasionally happen. On 1 July 1989 I came upon a hind at a height of about 400 metres near the summit of Cores Mountain. Both of her hind legs were paralysed and folded up underneath her; they did not trail behind. She dragged herself forward with her front legs, occasionally falling sideways, and once on to her back. When she saw me, she pulled herself forward with her front legs and, by flattening herself out, hid in tall tussocks of purple moor-grass. Later that night I telephoned a six-digit grid reference of her position to the wildlife staff of the park. Nevertheless, so effectively had she concealed herself that she was not found until about 36 hours later. By that time she had already been torn to pieces by foxes, ravens and grey crows – the scavengers of the hills. Seven days later, when I returned to the site, all that was left was a brown stain on the mountain grasses, some bunches of hair, a few ribs already picked clean, and her skull and jawbones, still attached to part of her backbone.

She was young, about two years of age, and had therefore become pregnant at about 15 months. Her approximate age can be deduced from the order in which the teeth cut the gum and from the degree of wear which they have sustained. As she had no milk teeth, she was above one year old and, because her third molars had not yet appeared, she was under three.

I discussed the incident with a veterinary surgeon. It is likely that she was suffering from *obturator paralysis*, a condition occasioned by her calf being stuck inside her for some time and pressing against the obturator nerve, which paralysed her hind legs. Whereas it is possible that she may have been carrying twin calves, this is rare in red deer, and has not been described in Killarney, though twin foetuses have been recorded in sika deer in County Wicklow[4]. The above episode illustrates how unforgiving the wild character of the Kerry hills can be, and how swiftly corpses disappear there.

The new-born calf must struggle to its feet and start suckling, and a hind's milk is sufficient to strengthen it within a day. The calf is already equipped for life on the open mountainside. Its eyes are open; it is covered with a protective fur; and its first coat is dappled, which gives it a measure of protective camouflage, provided it remains absolutely still. The ability to lie immobile, coupled with the generally accepted fact that for the first few days of its life a deer calf possesses little or no scent, is probably its greatest natural protection on the open mountain. In addition, the mother hides her calf under grass tussocks or heather clumps. The calf's ears are already large in relation to its face, and its hearing, a crucial sense for the red deer, is obviously already of great importance as soon as it is born.

The calf is an endearing animal at this early stage and, if found, its colourful spotted coat and large black eyes are difficult to resist. (A calf's eyes, like that of its parents, are a lustrous very dark brown, but can appear black. Some of the red deer on the Killarney hills, however, possess blond, straw-coloured eyes, which can be present in both hinds and stags. A hind with such a bleached eye colour can have a following calf which has the much more typical dark eyes. It is a small minority of the red deer on the hill that carry these lightly coloured eyes, and I have not observed it in the lowland animals.) However, any calf so found is very unlikely to have been abandoned and is best left untouched; far better to take only a photograph, and leave it to the expert care of its mother, who is probably watching from a distance and will return to her offspring in due course.

Some mountain-born calves of one or two days old that were weighed in the 1970s averaged about 4 to 5 kilograms, but much larger young are also born. For instance a female calf, weighed just after birth on 13 June 1987, weighed 8.8 kilograms. In the first half of June, when calving peaks, researchers endeavour to mark as many calves as possible, by placing a brightly coloured plastic tag on one or both ears (usually the left for females and the right for males), so as to help identify individual animals in future. Combinations of five different colours and five different patterns are used. As some tags are lost, recent practice has been to apply two tags, one to each ear (but with the larger tag on the left for females and right for males).

The new-born calf has two whorls of hair on its forehead, which are present on both males and females. These whorls are the sites of the future pedicles on the male: the columns of bone which will subsequently develop and on which his future antlers will grow. Antlers do not develop in females, though the whorls of hair remain.

Life on the open mountain advances quickly. The young calf is soon up and running. It acquires strength and swiftness and after about two days it can outrun a man, though it may not as yet run with its mother and the herd. It lies concealed, curled up in its lair of grass or heather, head stretched out on the ground, motionless but conscious of all that is going on around it. It will lie absolutely still until eye contact is made with the observer. Then it explodes into action and races off. Its mother, never very far away and always alert, soon appears and will take it swiftly uphill and away.

Parent hinds with calves hidden at this time generally feed alone. Deer moult their pelage in spring and autumn, but a hind on the hill which is lactating (in milk) may still retain her pale, straw-coloured winter coat and stand out against the green hillside. Nevertheless, to spot a lactating hind returning to her offspring is a difficult and protracted task, although this is a traditional way to locate a calf. The hind is in her home range and can use every fold and undulation of the hill to her advantage, so that she literally seems to disappear before one's eyes. The solitary hind continues to graze and move forward normally, only approaching the concealed calf at the very last moment, and then usually stopping 10 to 20 metres from the place of concealment, to check the whole hillside with a swift look around. She moves the last few metres very cautiously, and finally, when about 2 to 3 metres away, the calf jumps up and runs to her, perhaps at a vocal signal that one cannot hear on the hill.

Such extreme wariness, common in all truly wild animals, is a necessary protection against predation, and the young calf, though carefully hidden, has many enemies. A weak calf, either at birth or shortly afterwards, is vulnerable to grey crows and ravens, which will pick out its eyes and leave it helpless to its fate. Parent hinds are well aware of this threat. On one occasion, on 7 June, during peak calving time, a solitary hind grazing on the Ferta slopes suddenly became alert, turned her ears forward, and began running, downhill at first, then diagonally across the hillside for about 600 metres, until she came swiftly up to where a group of four ravens were on the ground, near some sheep. The hind ran at them, driving them off. Two of the ravens landed again about 50 metres away, but the hind followed these up, again charging at them with her head lowered and neck stretched out towards them, and chased them off. These two ravens then also flew away. The hind looked about; then walked back to where the four ravens had been, near the sheep. Immediately a calf stood up – it was one of those already tagged a few days before and easily identified. The hind now drove off her yearling, who had followed her and was also about to approach the calf, and she herself then went to her calf very slowly and cautiously, and commenced licking it. Soon mother and calf were moving about, the calf starting to suckle. The hind's action implied that she had a mental picture of where her calf lay concealed on the exposed, featureless mountain slope while she was over 600 metres away, and that she had considered the ravens on the ground near by a threat to her offspring.

Foxes have growing cubs to feed at this time of year and regularly patrol the mountain. A fox was recorded attacking a male sika calf in the park in August 1987[5]. I have several times witnessed a hind becoming alarmed at the sight of a fox at this time, and sometimes seen her move threateningly towards it, with foreleg raised to strike. Hinds and calves are still frightened occasionally when a hen harrier, quartering the hillside, suddenly appears over a crest of hill above them. In the historical records, a description is given of eagles attacking deer calves in County Mayo[6], and the echo of fear from large birds of prey still seems to linger.

This is also the time of increased tourist activity on the hill, with consequent disturbances, particularly by loose dogs. A more recent and serious threat to the red deer and their calves at this and other times is the prevalence of motorcycle scrambling. In my experience, when 20 motor-cycles come roaring up the hill slopes, deer are up and running 3 kilometres away. Apart from the obvious disturbances and threat to wildlife, such intrusion into the tranquillity and serenity of the mountains is intolerable, and it contravenes park regulations.

This is the time when some of the parent hinds may be seen *twirling*, an activity which I have so far failed to find described in any of the literature on red deer, and I have observed it only in the mountain population. In twirling – and there may be several bouts – the hind turns clockwise, rapidly and tightly within her own length. In effect, she pivots on her hind legs, using her forelegs to spin around. She appears fully alert, with neck kept upright, head erect, and ears cocked forward. Twirling was seen only in lactating hinds that were disturbed, and mostly when their calves were hidden, although also when the calves were up and running with the herd.

It was only some milk hinds, about one in five of those observed, that twirled. It appeared to be brought on by a human intruder appearing suddenly and close to a grazing milk hind that had a calf hidden away somewhere in the vicinity. The nearer to the hind that the intruder appeared, the greater the number of revolutions per bout. In a close encounter, a hind may twirl up to 12 or 14 times in her first bout. Then she may slow down, pause for a moment, and then resume twirling. Once, a hind with calf, who had spun six times in her first bout, then went deliberately to the top of a hillock, and twirled again, 13 times. This time she revolved so rapidly, and in such tight clockwise circles, that she leaned inwards, towards her right, and at an angle of about 30 degrees from the vertical. On stopping, she appeared quite normal, neither confused nor dizzy, and cantered away followed by her calf.

Sometimes a hind was seen to run off for about 30 to 40 metres, stop, and briefly survey the intruder, then start spinning once more, after which she galloped for a further short distance and commenced to twirl yet again. On occasion the hind ran out of sight or was observed joining a more distant group of deer. During the peak calving period, the twirling hinds, after making off, stayed around at a distance of about 200 metres, keeping a close watch on the intruder.

It is difficult to provide a satisfactory explanation for twirling. It appears to be confined to the mountain red deer. It has never been seen, either by myself or any of the other six observers who have witnessed it, in the sika deer which occupy the same range. It is tempting to regard it as an effort to lure away the intruder, similar to the behaviour of some ground-nesting birds, which apparently feign a broken wing for this purpose. There is an element of confusion observable in some instances of twirling. For example the calf, if up and running with the hind, stands some way off, looking confused. In one instance, on 20 July 1985, the hind had already twirled 14 times in one bout. Then she moved off a little and twirled again, bumping into her calf and two-year-old follower in the process, and pushing them aside. However, in all other cases observed, the hind completed twirling upright and alert, appearing fully in control, undistressed, apparently without ill effects, and was able to lope away with the normal long, striding gait typical of the red deer.

A Canadian biologist has described to me that a reaction something similar to twirling can be induced in an inexperienced hind (a hind after her first pregnancy) by imitating the panic-squeal of a calf, and can be brought on by introducing an "artificial predator" – a trained and carefully controlled dog – into the calving area[7].

In researching the literature, I have discovered other instances of deer appearing to try to lead away a predator. For example, there is a reference to a mother American elk going to considerable lengths to lure off a bear[8]. And, in France in the 1750s, a report on observations of red deer and their reaction to wolves outside Paris[9] states that hinds with young possess "a tender and bold anxiety which makes the mother cross the path of the dogs to lead them away from her young; at first a faint flight and a prompt return when the danger has passed by". Wolves were finally exterminated in Ireland in the mid to late 1700s, and the wilds of Kerry may have harboured some of the last of them. It is just possible that the effort to lure away a predator has survived as a relic behaviour in the isolated population of the Killarney red deer, and that it manifests itself at the peak calving period in some of the parent hinds.

By mid-June births have peaked. But there are always exceptions. An early calf is sometimes born in the second half of May, and in many years there are also late births. A few young calves, still in their spotted coats, are found as late as mid-October in both the uplands and lowlands. Such youngsters must have been conceived in the previous January or February, and dropped in late August or early September, for the juvenile coat is retained for from four to six weeks.

Thus begins both the year and life cycle of the wild red deer.

The calf is born into a time of plenty and also into the security of the red deer family. This is, typically, the parent hind, her calf of the year, followed by her yearling, and sometimes two-year-old female offspring, for some mountain hinds skip a year in breeding. Yearling and two-year-old males (young stags), if they have remained with the parent hind, will generally bring up the rear. This is the observed order of progression as deer go about the hill, changing feeding grounds, and moving from high to low pastures. If there is a major disturbance and the family panics and takes flight, then the calf will stick tightly behind its mother, bouncing along at her heels, whether the others scatter or not.

As July advances, deer families coalesce and form larger groups. Bands of up to 20 red deer, composed of three or four families, can be seen on the hillsides at this time. Within these bands the calves have a secure position. This is very evident when the hinds lie up to cud. They select open country, generally on a gently sloping hillside, and settle down in a rough circle, within which the calf or calves lie, necks stretched out and heads on the ground, sleeping. As the hinds face outwards, all angles of approach are covered by hearing, smell, and sight.

The calves, now two to three weeks old, are already cropping the vegetation. At only three days, they are known to nibble earth, and this is one way in which the bacteria and micro-fauna, essential to the break-down of plant cell walls, are ingested into the rumen, enabling them to commence the lifelong process of chewing the cud. A calf also acquires micro-fauna through suckling or licking its mother after she has lain on the ground[10].

Calves are now a joy to watch. They stand upright on hind legs, front legs tucked tight against their stomachs, and peer over the tall tussocks of mountain grasses. They stoop delicately to lap up water from bog pools on the high mountain ledges. And they play. Calves play with each other, with their elder sisters, and not infrequently mother joins in. In isolated families, play is sometimes initiated by the female yearling. Among larger groups, where as many as eight or 10 calves come together, play mostly takes the form of chasing. The calves run and bound in circles or figures of eight, winding around and in amongst the hinds as they lie cudding. It is impossible to witness these bouts of play without accepting that the participants are enjoying themselves. The areas where red deer lie up and play are carefully selected: mostly on broad, open and level benches, high up on the rolling exposed ridges, where visibility is possible in all directions and where rising air currents waft scents of danger. Sometimes play spills into and amongst the groups of stags which also occupy the same high ridges and often lie up near by. When this occurs, my experience is that the stags, in general, tolerate the gambols of the youngsters.

Red deer calves lose their spots within four to six weeks of birth so that, by the end of July, almost all calves on the hill have changed their juvenile coats, though I once noted a strong calf with almost all its spots gone as early as 4 July. Calves are now running strongly with the hinds, and still enjoy the privileged and protected position of being next to their mothers. Even strong calves cannot yet keep up with the herd in prolonged flight, although they have acquired the long loping gait of the adult by this time. In a prolonged flight the calf gallops closely behind its mother, but when out of range of danger, generally about 2 kilometres, the calf suddenly disappears. It is either pressed down into the heather or tall grasses by its mother, who continues to run, frequently changing direction, or it drops of its own accord. This action is so fast that it is difficult to analyse; the calf appears to drop instantaneously into high vegetation, perhaps at some signal far too swift and subtle for us to observe.

Even when not in flight, the calf still enjoys its privileged place. A good example of this was seen one July when an undisturbed group of two or three families was crossing a stream. The leading, dominant hind, who had a calf, took precedence. She splashed across, closely followed by the calf at her heels. Then came the next mother, again with her calf immediately following, and so on. The rest of the group waited about until all mothers and calves had passed over, before crossing themselves, all in single file.

A calf of four to six weeks old is not as easy a prey as is generally assumed, as was illustrated by an incident which happened some years ago in Killarney. The park wildlife staff had been hand-rearing a male sika calf which had been injured by a car on the Killarney-Kenmare road. It was kept in an open yard, adjacent to woodlands. When a border collie went into the yard, the calf immediately became fully alert and, without hesitating, attacked the sheepdog, striking it smartly on the face with its sharp front hoof. The dog turned and fled.

By mid-July hinds are in their full summer coats, shorter and redder than their winter ones, although a lactating hind may retain her winter pelage, bleached by the elements. This can happen because the burden of a previous severe winter, coupled with the drain of pregnancy and the demands of lactation, may inhibit or delay the yearly moult and regrowth. Hinds that have not produced young are noticeable for the richness and sleekness of their red summer coats; such individuals are known as "yeld" hinds or, in Killarney, more commonly as "dry" hinds. However, all richly coloured female adults are not necessarily yeld. From tagging studies, we now know that some of the Muckross lowland hinds migrate to the uplands to calve, and these are invariably a glossy, rich red-brown. Red deer are never so "red" as they are now, a hue often like that of a freshly opened chestnut, although there is a good deal of colour variation from animal to animal.

The hinds are now in the serious business of laying down fat reserves for the coming winter, as well as continuing to provide milk for the current year's calves. Increased temperatures and long hours of daylight are put to advantage, as the animals are increasingly active now, and for longer periods. From various published studies of other red deer[11], it has been established that both appetite and food intake are significantly greater than in winter.

The deer's day is a series of activities commencing with food gathering, then retiring to a secure position for lying up and cud chewing, followed by more grazing, and more cud chewing. Cudding sites are carefully selected. The direction of the wind is important, as it brings with it scents and sounds of danger. Red deer lie up with their backs to the wind and generally just below the brow of a hill, with a large open area spread out before and below them. Thus they are not only sheltered by the hilltop, but they can also see the countryside in front and hear and smell any danger that may come from behind them.

If the day is hot and sunny, they may seek out the shade of tall grass and bracken where they are fully hidden. In the evening a bracken covered hillside can suddenly become alive with deer, as they emerge from amongst foliage for the evening-to-dusk feed. In summer the late evening feed is an excellent time to watch red deer on the hill, and this is particularly so if it has been a day of soft rain with the evening turning fine, as can often happen in Killarney. Then the deer move out and graze eagerly on the lush wet grasses. Such grazing is neither continuous nor intensive, but appears to be selective: four to six bites here, then 10 to 20 paces forward, a few more bites there, and so on.

Fine summers are rare in Killarney. More often the mountain summer is cool, clouded, windy and wet. Sometimes it can be very wet. It varies from a light mountain mist to a downpour, but given the oceanic influence on the Killarney mountains, there are many summers where scarcely a day passes without some precipitation. It can also be surprisingly cold. On 8 July 1989 a north-east wind on the exposed slopes had accentuated the chilling effects of a scudding white mist, and a group of 19 red hinds and calves were crowded into a hollow, sheltering from the wind. Such a pattern of weather has a discernible effect on subsequent performance (survival and reproductive success) of the upland red deer. In the meantime daily life goes on. The deer move out and feed at their usual times even in the heaviest downpour, rumps to the wind and rain.

The family life of the red deer is not without its squabbles and, indeed, external irritations in the form of parasites[12], and disturbance. In July and early August, fly worry can be a considerable annoyance. The deer frequently shake their heads and flap their ears to shake off the insects, their tails being far too short for this purpose. To avoid flies and midges, a hind will stretch out her long neck on the ground and bury her face, and particularly her nose, in the high grasses of the mountain summer. This gives only temporary relief; soon the deer are on their feet again, shaking their heads and moving on, seeking a windy spot. They are also troubled by lice and ticks and repeatedly turn around to bite and nibble at their backs, sides and around the groin, or to scratch behind their ears with their hooves. They also seek out traditional scratching posts, for example a few larch trees which grow on the steep sides of one of the mountain streams. In places some of these are not only rubbed clean of bark, but the exposed wood is also polished from years of neck scratching. Ultimately, the only escape from the flies and midges is a strong wind, and in the summer red deer seek the exposed high ground, going right up to the summits.

There are also family tiffs, especially amongst hinds, who establish dominance by standing on their hind legs and boxing with their forefeet. The fight is short but vicious; a hind's forefoot is a lethal weapon with a sharp hoof which can inflict a serious wound. These encounters are sometimes seen on the mountains, and seem to occur principally where many deer groups crowd into a particularly favoured feeding area. Disputes of this kind are also seen in the lowlands.

Hinds wallow regularly throughout the summer in holes which they dig with their forefeet in the soft blanket bog, and which quickly fill with water, creating a slurry of peat. Some of these sites are traditional and are used year after year. Wallowing is normally a solitary activity, but sometimes hinds do it together, with up to four animals getting into the same large pool and covering themselves up to their eyes in wet black muck, as they rub their faces, necks, throats and chins in the sludge, sometimes with a calf looking on from the edge. Sometimes wallowing is playful amongst the young hinds. Their whole bodies are submerged in the wet peat, with much twitching of ears and shaking of heads, and then bucking out playfully, and jumping back in again. On the open mountain such behaviour can only be seen from a distance, except in really exceptional circumstances. At the slightest indication of intrusion or human presence the deer are off, and vanish over the hills. Calves also wallow, in among hinds in the same pool, but this may simply be in imitation of their mothers. It is generally supposed that wallowing is to get rid of external parasites. In late spring and early summer, when the winter coat is coming off, long coat hairs float about in bunches on the dark pool's surface.

Now that the calves are strong and running alongside their mothers, suckling takes place out in the open and at an opportune time that the hind permits. Sometimes it appears as if there is some subtle signal at which the calf rushes to its mother and commences suckling. While nursing, the calf is almost always positioned at the hind's side with its rump alongside her face. In this position the hind can attend to cleaning and licking the calf's anal region, the calf facilitating this by keeping its tail bolt upright throughout. The mother also accomplishes anal grooming when the calf grazes in front of her. Such grooming removes the mucous which results from a diet of milk and which might otherwise clog the anus.

Suckling is a vigorous activity, and when several months old a strong calf can lift its mother off the ground as it bunts with its head to initiate the process. Nursing lasts about one or two minutes, when the hind firmly signals that that is enough by walking away. Often the calf will follow, attempting to start again from behind. This is discouraged quickly with a kick. Suckling also occurs at night as witnessed during night censuses in the Killarney lowlands.

Though the calves are strong by now, parent hinds are still wary and maintain an increased flight distance (the critical distance at which they will run from a threat). On the open mountain any intrusion is sensed at least a kilometre away, and long before the source of danger is within half a kilometre, hinds and calves are away, leading the rest of the group and galloping off, mostly uphill to the safety of the higher slopes. When a possible threat is identified, several types of alarm signals may be given by the hind, alerting other deer within hearing and sight. A nursing mother is immediately alert at the slightest unusual sound or scent, and she focuses ears, eyes and nose at the source, neck held up straight and stiff, ears cocked forward, and her whole body tense and quivering. The hind may alarm-bark: a short, sharp bark which carries far and alerts other deer within hearing. If the source of the threat cannot be clearly identified, she continues barking at intervals of a few minutes, and may go on for about half an hour before finally settling down again if the intrusion disappears. The hind may additionally signal an alarm by stamping her forefoot sharply on the ground, and then stand with the leg lifted and curled, ready to strike again. Sometimes she gives this alarm signal with her hind foot, and will stand with a hind leg splayed to the side, which is, incidentally, a characteristic alarm signal of caribou[13]. The hind's long elegant neck is put to good advantage when she is on the lookout. If a sound comes from behind, she can turn her head through 180 degrees to survey the countryside, without moving her body, thus effectively achieving vision through a full 360 degrees simply by turning her neck alternately from side to side.

From about mid-July onwards, family groups tend to coalesce more and more. This is the beginning of the spectacular summer aggregations, which are a feature of the Killarney hills. An aggregation is a gathering of family groups of wild red deer which herd together in numbers far in excess of those seen throughout the rest of the year. They assemble on the more level and open expanses of bogland, where the approach of an intruder is made doubly difficult, and where the deer have an unrestricted view. It is called an aggregation simply because that is what it is rather than a cohesive social unit. This is very evident when an aggregation splits up. It fragments into the original family groups again.

The advantage of these aggregations is probably greater security from predators. There is safety in numbers, and each deer has a better chance of survival from the collective watchfulness of many individuals. Stag groups may sometimes be included, though stags tend to keep to themselves and to one side of the main assemblage. An aggregation is a wonderful sight, as impressive as it is unusual, especially as one is unlikely to see a group larger than about 15 to 20 on the mountains for the rest of the year. The greatest number of deer which I have observed together was 164 head, in 1983. That probably represented about one-third of all the wild red deer in the Killarney uplands at that time.

Many activities take place within the aggregation. There is the normal grazing, calf play, lying up and cudding. A special feature is sexual play. A yearling hind will try and mount another hind; this is fairly common. Sometimes a calf will try and mount its mother; this occurs more frequently later, when the calf is about four months old. By far the most unusual activity of this type which I have observed was a red calf mounting an adult sika buck, on 12 August 1989. The buck, while grazing, had moved in among some red hinds and calves that were lying up and cudding. The red calf approached and mounted the sika on five consecutive occasions. It appeared to be an effort at play. What was astonishing was the tolerance and docility of the sika. He stood still during the mountings and just once turned his head to look back at the red calf while it was mounting.

There is also much vocalising by the deer within the aggregation. On a quiet summer afternoon, when they are unaware of one's presence, there are many types of calls which are rarely heard at other times of the year, even incipient roars from the stags, although these are but a poor semblance of the full-bodied roar of the rut to come.

An aggregation seems to have a magnetism of its own. I once saw a group of eight stags leave a high mountain ridge and gallop down for over 2 kilometres, apparently just to join a much larger group of stags who were feeding out on the open bogland below them, and adjacent to a greater aggregation of deer near by. In this instance, apparently the stags had been spontaneously attracted by the sight of the large number of animals below; there was no other interference or apparent explanation for their behaviour.

Such magnetism is also evident when watching an aggregation beginning to form. A group of deer, perhaps five or six, will suddenly set off at a run across the hillside for no apparent reason. As they pass, many other deer seem to simply materialise from the ground – they just stand up from where they have been lying. Once initiated, the process gathers momentum. Before one's eyes the numbers grow. One such incident ended up with at least 55 deer, all closely bunched, eventually halting and then remaining together.

Within the aggregation, which at times may be spread out over the open moor in a loosely knit series of smaller groups, it is obvious that one of the older, dominant hinds is the ultimate leader, not only of her own family, but apparently of all of the deer present. This was evident on one occasion when an unhurried move to another feeding area was initiated by a mature hind. She got up and walked away, slowly and deliberately, followed in single file by her calf of the year, then by her older daughter. Several paces behind came another hind, again with her calf, and then her follower. Gradually the others rose and walked after them, all behind one another, so that eventually the entire aggregation formed one long line of over 100 individuals, dawdling leisurely across the hill in single file to fresh pasture. The entire performance and relaxed, deliberate progress was a magnificent sight. A slow walking pace, in single file, is the most efficient method of travel across mountain slopes, demanding the least energy and conserving that energy for future survival in the hard times ahead.

This is the time of maximum human impact on the hills, when walkers, mountain climbers, and the ever growing number of tourists in Killarney visit the park, anxious to see the red deer. Exceptionally, some visitors appear to cause no apparent disturbance, as I have observed walkers to pass within about 400 metres of red deer which scarcely ceased feeding. Deer appear to be able to sense whether or not walkers have seen them, and very often casual visitors to the mountains do not spot the deer which, nevertheless, are watching them all the time. However, the situation quickly alters if the intruders are noisy and undisciplined, especially if they bring loose dogs with them.

Dogs at large cause deer aggregations to fragment and scatter. The stags group together and gallop off in a closely packed bunch, with every individual fending for himself, although dominance is still evident in that the older, more experienced animals stay well within the centre of the crowd, shoving the younger, subordinate stags out to the edge, where they are more vulnerable. Hinds and calves break up into smaller and smaller parties, parties that may eventually be reduced to one or two family units of hind, calf and followers. When the deer have sufficiently distanced themselves from the disturbance, the pace slackens, and the animals resume their normal and more efficient mode of travel: single file.

But fragmentation is far from orderly, and sometimes in the general mêlée there is considerable mixing, with some calves being separated from their mothers. If, on regrouping, a hind is approached by a stray calf, she will lash out viciously with her forefoot. A hind is equally violent on other occasions, as for example when she strikes out with her forefoot if approached by a sika calf in the mountains. While a red deer calf may be temporarily lost after the sudden break-up of an aggregation, a parent hind seems to know her offspring, even when in full flight. On one such occasion a hind made a prodigious leap simply to avoid colliding with her own calf.

Not all the red deer crowd into aggregations. There are always those who do not join the herd, and even when an aggregation is at its peak, individual hinds with calves can be seen far off grazing alone, sometimes on rugged terrain, as for example the steep, north-facing cliffs and ledges of Torc. These "loners" seem oblivious to the magnetism of the crowd.

The importance of increased food intake for hind, calf and stag continues throughout the summer. By mid-July the mountain vegetation has attained full summer growth, and the deer graze greedily. The forage is essentially native: mountain grasses, sedges, rushes, myrtle, heather and furze, as well as some browse from the few available trees of birch, oak, holly, alder and whitehorn. The red deer also eat bracken. They crop the tender, green, growing tips early in summer, and also the mature plant up to the end of August. This is a slow, neat, and selective process, in contrast to the biting munch when grass is being gathered. The hind searches for a green frond, passing up withered ones, and then neatly nips it off, breaking it with a jerk of her head and drawing it slowly into her mouth as she chews. Likewise a calf, now almost three months old, will also browse bracken fronds. Though it must sometimes stretch its neck to the limit to reach the green tops, it nevertheless can also find young fronds lower down.

After food gathering comes cudding, a process that occupies a considerable amount of a red deer's late mornings, middays, and early afternoons. A hind has commenced to cud even as she begins to lie down. Then there are 50 to 70 strokes of the jaws as she chews the cud, followed by a swallow. Then another wad is regurgitated, and the chewing is renewed. The process can last for up to two hours, and can become boring to the deer watcher. However, the hinds are alert at all times, and at any disturbance they are up and away, calves following.

Thus the young red deer goes through the summer, rapidly gaining strength and size, in the company and security of its mother and the family group. By three months it is well on its way to its first thick winter coat. It is time now, however, to give some thought to the stags.

Plate 1   Young red hind amidst the molinia *tussocks*

Plate 2   Red deer calf mounting sika buck, Cloughfune area

Plate 3   Red deer hind with emerging foetus on Ferta

Plate 4   *Calving problems: red deer hind with* obturator paralysis, *her hind legs crippled, Cores Mountain*

Plate 5   *Sika calf. The whorls of hair on its forehead are where future antlers will develop, if a male*

Plate 6   The large ears area in relation to its head is a feature of a red deer calf

Plate 7   Red deer hind on Cores Mountain searches for intruders by turning her head 180 degrees

Plate 8   The typical alarm signal of an alert hind: her hind leg raised ready to strike

Plate 9   Red hind in full summer coat; red is a term used for a variety of shades of reddish-brown

Plate 10   Stag in velvet signals his intentions to strike

Plate 11   Growing antlers, in velvet, of mountain stag on Cores Mountain

Plate 12   In the lowland pastures, magpie searching for flies on red stag's antlers in velvet

Plate 13   The summer pelage of sika, unlike that of adult red deer, is spotted

Plate 14 Part of the red deer herd, summer aggregation on Cores Mountain

Plate 15 Two of the lowland stags in velvet

II

High Summer

Éistecht co moch i rRos Grencha
  frisin damraid,
coicetal na cúach don fhidbaid
  ar brúach shamraid.

Listening early in Ross Grencha to the stags, and to cuckoos
calling from the woodland, on the brink of summer.

Irish poem, c. 1000 A.D.[1]

By early summer stags are either growing a new pair of antlers or preparing to grow a first pair. The young male at first grows *pedicles*, two columns which sprout upwards from the frontal bone of his forehead. The whorls of hair, present at birth, unravel as the columns enlarge, and the pedicles are covered by this coat of skin and hair[2]. Some young stags begin to acquire them before they are twelve months old. Such early development is common in the Killarney lowlands, where forage grows over limestone rocks, and is therefore rich in calcium. Furthermore, the winters are less severe. In the Killarney mountains pedicles generally do not begin to appear until the end of summer, in September, when the stag is about fifteen months old.

In the mountain herd the first *heads* (antlers), at the end of their second summer, are short, upright spikes, sometimes with a simple bifurcation just above where the pedicle ends and the antler commences, called a *brow tine*. In the terminology of antlers the word tine is essentially synonymous with *point*. These antlers of bone are covered with skin and hair, called *velvet*. The stag's first head thus carries two or four points. In the lowlands, these first spikes are much larger and develop earlier, even in the animal's first year. An exceptional lowland youngster may have a further branching higher up on the main beam of his antler, giving him six points for his first head.

Older stags have more elaborate antlers, which generally begin to grow from early March. By summer they are well developed, looking larger than they actually are as the velvet gives them a furry, swollen appearance. The antlers of mountain stags in their third summer are more elaborately branched, carrying perhaps four or occasionally six points. The next tine which develops along the main beam, above the brow tine, is not infrequently the *tray* tine in Killarney mountain stags. Between that and the brow tine, a further one, called the *bey* tine, may develop in future years, though on the Killarney hills many stags may never acquire it. By his second year, a lowland stag has already developed six or eight points. Some stags that have overwintered in the Killarney lowlands move up on to the hill in the following summer. Consequently, there is sometimes the confusing spectacle of two young stags grazing close together on a hillside, one with the short simple spikes of an uplander, the other with the much longer spikes of the lowlander, perhaps complete with brow tines, and twice as large as those of his mountain counterpart.

Stags that are three or four years old have, in general, more elaborate antlers again. In the mountains the top points generally branch out above the tray tine before the bey tine develops, if it does at all. This can give the animal a head of eight points or, not infrequently, nine points, as there is much variation in antler shape and size, and an even number of points on each side is not a regular pattern.

Five to six-year-old stags are already nearly full grown. These have yet more elaborate antlers, and the number of points may be anything from nine to about 14. Still older stags, over 9 or 10 years and past their prime, characteristically have antlers of the same shape, but not necessarily the same number of points. The latter may increase, with smaller tines on the top, known as *crown* points, up to a head of 15 or 16 points, the normal maximum seen on the Kerry mountains. Larger and more elaborate antlers with up to 18 points are carried by exceptional stags in the lowlands. *Hummels*, stags that never grow antlers but mature and breed successfully, are unknown in Killarney in my experience, although an account in 1949[3], based on local recollection, mentioned a few of them having occurred there. The possibility of a sika hummel in Killarney was recorded in 1984[4].

Since antler shapes and sizes are influenced not only by the animal's age but also by his general health, the quality of his food and his inherited characteristics, the number of antler points cannot provide an accurate indication of a stag's age – at best they are only a rough guide. Also, if an antler is accidentally damaged in growth, while still soft and vulnerable, its final shape and size will be deformed. It has also been shown in Scottish studies[5] that as deer density increases, antlers become lighter[6]. Despite this, the most frequently discussed aspect of antlers, and probably the most topical in general discussion on red deer, is the question of a stag's age.

As the number of points increases up to a certain age, it is a common enough assumption that a stag with fewer points must be younger. However, some stags may never go beyond eight points. Others in contrast may go as high as 16 points. As the animal ages the antlers grow less vigorously, and some points are lost. Such antlers are said to have *gone back*. Those points which remain become shorter, blunter and eventually, in exceptional cases, all that may be left is the main beam. An old stag with such antlers is known as a *switch*. It takes many years of prolonged observation and experience to judge a wild stag's age by sight, and even then any of us can be mistaken. Many records in the shooting literature tell of stags shot "by mistake", on the assumption that the animal was much older or in poorer condition than it was eventually found to be when the carcass was examined[7].

Young stags stay with the family group up to about their second year, after which they live in separate all-male groups, but on occasion, of course, tag along with the summer aggregations. The stag herd is not structured on family lines, as is the hind group. Dominance is determined by maturity, general health and condition, and body weight and size. Where there is no disturbance, stags traverse the mountain slopes in much the same way as hinds – in single file, the dominant stags invariably taking up the rear.

Dominance is asserted in many ways, sometimes by a gesture of the head and antlers, or simply by a look. When the stag group is undisturbed, a look can be enough to set the younger stags leading the rest off to a different pasture. Signals are not always so subtle. Squabbles flare up, and in high summer, when the stags' antlers are still growing and tender, a dispute is settled by the opponents rearing up on their hind legs and boxing with their forefeet. The hierarchy of dominance is a loose one, which can change as some stags leave one herd and join another, but an order of dominance is quickly settled and there is little waste of energy, a precious commodity in an environment as demanding as the open mountain. Arguments over patches of grazing may also be resolved by one animal, usually the larger, kicking at the intruder. A red deer, whether male or female, usually signals its intention to kick by stretching up its neck and flattening its ears back against its head, so that the light-coloured tufts of hair within the ears are prominent. On many occasions it was obvious that the animal potentially at the receiving end read the signal and moved swiftly to avoid the kick. One of the illustrations shows where the flattened ears of the aggressor have been interpreted, and the threatened animal is already rearing up and away from the expected kick.

The upland environment is now at its most benign, and the stags, like the hinds and calves, take full advantage of the lush growth to accumulate body fat for the coming rut and for the following winter, and also to provide for their antlers, which are still developing. Indeed, these are one of the fastest growing bony structures known, and the demand on the stag's body, especially the mature stags with large and elaborate antlers, is severe. Studies have shown[8] that, over their period of growth (approximately three months), food intake cannot keep pace with the quantities of minerals required, especially in mountain habitats. The deficiency is made up by a seasonal withdrawal from the animal's own bone reserves. In the mountains, stags chew cast antlers and bones left on the hill, seeking minerals. Similarly, a pregnant hind cannot always supply sufficient nutrients from mountain forage to provide for her growing foetus, and she makes good the shortfall in the same way, as well as utilising some of her own body reserves.

In June, stag herds on the hill are rarely greater than 12 to 15 individuals. It is not unusual to see a group of just two or three stags, banding together and living generally high up, where they can get relief from flies and midges. The growing antler in velvet is generally abuzz with a swarm of flies, particularly if there is the slightest cut or nick, where the insects cluster in black clouds on to the oozing blood. The growing bone surface and the covering of velvet are rich in blood vessels, and as the bone has not yet hardened, the antler is soft, very tender, and easily damaged. Because of this, the stag cannot rid himself of flies by threshing shrubs. Instead he seeks out softer vegetation: fronds of bracken, or the growing tips of heather, into which he gently plunges his antlers, endeavouring to shake off his tormentors. Some lowland stags enjoy a remarkable and mutually beneficial partnership with magpies in the matter of relief from flies. I and others have observed a magpie alight on a stag's back; then fly up to perch momentarily on his antlers; pick off flies; and return to the stag's back; only to repeat the performance again and again.

Sometimes a close relationship is evident between a younger and an older stag. The two appear to be inseparable at this time, feeding together on the hillside, lying up together, and staying apart from other stag groups. In such partnerships the older stag is frequently past his prime and already beginning to deteriorate in strength, weight, and antler.

Stags are alert and will bark an alarm similar to hinds, but the bark has a lower and deeper timbre, like a coughing grunt. Within stag groups there is much vocalisation, and sometimes a stag will roar. A summer roar is an incipient one, lacking the full volume and authority of the rutting roar, though exceptionally, a full-blooded roar can be heard. The earliest record I have of hearing such a full roar was on 8 June 1985.

By July the mature stags are in sleek summer coats, with necks that are still slender and lacking the thick mane which develops later. They range the entire mountains, going right up to the summit plateau of Mangerton (840 metres). And stags also wallow now, but less frequently than later in the summer when their antlers have hardened and the velvet is peeling off. As described in the previous chapter, stags often join summer aggregations in the latter part of July, when herds coalesce and increase in size. The largest group which I have observed was of 56 stags, on the 25 August 1984.

Towards the end of July the mountain vegetation is already beginning to change colour, as a russet tinge appears on the tips of the deer sedge. Into August, the daylight hours are noticeably shorter, and days and nights are colder. By now the mature stag's antlers are fully grown. The processes of shedding the velvet and the ritual of wallowing are beginning.

In August the antlers are cleaned; neck muscles swell; thick manes grow on throats; and aggression increases. August brings even more dramatic changes among the sika, which in the Killarney lowlands can begin to rut before the month is out, sometimes four to five weeks in advance of the red deer in the mountains.

Cleaning the antlers begins as soon as the velvet dries and shrivels. Stags begin to rub them against shrubs, furze bushes, rocks or along the ground, so that the dried skin begins to hang off in strips, peeling away and sometimes hanging down across the animal's face and into his eyes, causing annoyance and even alarm. Each stag cleans his antlers in his own way, and will go to considerable lengths to remove the dried velvet. The same applies to sika bucks. At this time a stag will emerge from a wallow with his body and legs dripping in black, glistening, wet peat, and with long strips of shrivelled skin festooning his antlers.

At first the exposed bone is reddish, but is soon stained dark brown, sometimes almost black, from wallowing and being plunged into the peat slurry and from being repeatedly rubbed against bushes and along the ground. The older animals clean their antlers first, by mid-August. A young stag may not strip his until September.

The year is changing. Daylight is decreasing daily; the nights grow even colder. The yellow spikes of bog asphodel have turned to brown seed heads; the white fluffy heads of bog cotton no longer flutter in the wind; grasses and sedges are already coloured by autumn, particularly at higher altitudes. Bell and ling heather are flowering purple on drier slopes, mixed with the yellow flowers of the dwarf furze. Soon that magnificent combination of purple and gold will carpet some hillsides, shining with a particularly deep and glowing intensity on soft wet days, and after heavy rain.

The stags too are changing. A mane of long dark hair develops on the enlarged muscles of the neck so that the animal eventually has an appearance of immense strength, concentrated around his forequarters, where the centre of gravity now so obviously lies. Aggression between stags is now open and is manifested by head shaking and short antler jabs and swipes. At this stage it is no more than that.

The sika are also changing, and as early as the second week in August, the brown, white-spotted coat of summer is darkening. The spots begin to fade and, particularly in mature bucks, the face and neck turn black, while the neck swells and mane grows. By the third week of August, the sika rut is sometimes already in progress in the woods of the Killarney lowlands.

The sika rut is heralded by the buck's wild whistle-scream, which penetrates the Killarney woodlands. Initially the whistle is a prolonged single note, but as the rut intensifies, the whistle is repeated three times. This sound is so characteristic that it cannot be mistaken for any other in the Kerry woods or mountains. Sika does are in oestrous (on heat) at this time, because with a gestation period of 32–34 weeks, sika calves have been recorded in the Killarney lowlands from as early as the following April.

In September the younger red stags, with antlers now clean, commence sparring among themselves. But this is not serious; it is obviously play. They spar gently, at first toying with their antlers, as if learning how to manipulate them precisely. They lower their heads, lock antlers, and playfully push each other about, from a few minutes to perhaps half an hour. Often they break off and graze, briefly, side by side. Then one initiates further wrestling by lowering his antlers and presenting them to his companion. So the fight-play continues sporadically among immature stags. Occasionally an older stag will stop grazing and stand, watching them as they spar.

By mid-September aggression is more marked. Mature stags in particular are increasingly intolerant of each other, and there are short chases as they attain peak condition. These animals will be the first to rut. Traditionally the first roars on the mountain are heard in the last week of September, but there is roaring in the lowlands as early as mid-September. When the first roaring is heard, the rut has commenced.

III

Autumn

Scél lem dúib:
  dordaid dam;
snigid gaim;
ro fáith sam;

I have tidings for you: the stag bells;
winter pours; summer has gone;

Irish poem, 9th century.[1]

Summer is indeed gone from the Killarney mountains when the roaring of the red stags ushers in the rut in October. The mature stags are now strong, fit and formidable-looking fighting machines, with the base of their necks as deep as the girth of their bodies behind the foreleg. Antlers are black from wallowing, and tine tips glisten white from threshing vegetation. A gland at the lower corner of the eye, the *preorbital* gland, exudes a rust coloured, resinous fluid. The faeces have changed from being discrete pellets to an amorphous round cake, like a miniature cow pat.

These stags have an aura of immense power as they break away from the male groups and begin to travel alone through the mountains. Their movement across the hills is a joy to watch. Differing entirely from the normal walking pace of single file in summer, it is now a long loping trot, the back slightly arched, the neck and head held forward. The animal moves at a canter, easily covering the mountain territory with surprising speed, and occasionally halting to roar.

He raises his head, lowers his antlers back along his flanks, and roars with mouth agape. When this is full throated and intense, the head goes right up with mouth open, and the antlers dip below the level of his back. While a travelling stag will roar anywhere, there is a tendency to use a hillock or the top of a rock outcrop, from where he can survey the country below. The roar of a stag is a wonderfully wild sound, echoing through the hills and, on still days, it carries a considerable distance. During the exceptionally calm October days of the 1986 rut, stags roaring on the Glena-

Shehy mountain slopes could be heard across the Killarney Valley in the Cores-Crinneagh area, a distance of about 5 kilometres. However, blustery strong winds with frequent showers of rain, and sometimes hail, are now common, and in such conditions a roar may carry over no more than half a kilometre.

The travelling stag is seeking to gather hinds to herd together for his *harem*, which he will then endeavour to possess exclusively. The amicable stag groups of summer are no more: they are now fragmented and dispersed. Every mature stag is a potential rival, and it is a case of every stag for himself. Mature stags are aggressive and deceptively swift in their movements. In my experience none is to be trusted from now on. Not only is he immensely strong and possessed of sharp pointed weapons, but his normal inclination to flee is largely suppressed by his urgency for the hinds and his willingness to fight.

The biggest stags are the first to hold hinds, defending them against the inevitable challengers. Until recently harems were generally small in the mountains. In those ruts which I observed in Killarney between 1965 and 1990, the maximum harem size which I recorded was 12, and the average about five, of which at least one hind was a yearling (which would be most unlikely to breed) and another a calf of the year. Harems could be much smaller. A stag, generally an old animal past his prime, could sometimes be seen to hold just one hind. However, in recent years harem size has increased, and one group of about 18 hinds was being herded by a stag – high on the slopes of Mangerton – in 1992. Such large groups are short lived. In a matter of a few days the numbers will have dwindled, as recounted below.

Large harems of 30–50 hinds described in red deer literature are, in my experience, unknown in Killarney. In the lowlands, some of the exceptionally large stags may now collect harems of up to 20 hinds, coinciding with an overall increase in the population.

Stags which succeed in holding hinds are referred to as *holders* or *stags in possession*, but traditionally in Killarney they are referred to simply as *master stags*. During the rut on the Killarney mountains, in my experience, the number of master stags might be no more than 30 to 35 animals. It is these master stags which control the rut. Younger stags, although capable of mating, are not large or strong enough to challenge the holders, and stags past their prime are unfit to challenge successfully. Nevertheless, these young and old stags are also on the move, wandering across the mountain slopes and roaring. But they must wait until the master stags are worn out before they can hope to take some of the hinds from them. By that time the holders will have already mated with the fittest hinds, who normally come on heat by the second and third week of October.

While in possession, stags will generally see to it that yearling males within the hind group are driven out. But this is not invariable, and during at least three separate ruts I have seen a master stag tolerate a yearling male within his harem. When ousted, the youngster hangs around at what he judges to be a safe distance, frightened and bewildered. One that I watched could be seen to actually flinch as the holder roared; his body tensed and his rump went down and inwards as if to tuck in his tail like a submissive dog. Such an outcast watches the holder constantly, and if the latter moves to the far side of the hill, or some distance away from his harem, the youngster runs back, endeavouring to rejoin his mother. Once the master stag senses this, he ejects the yearling again. A short run and threat gesture are sufficient to send him fleeing.

In a threat gesture, a stag lays his antlers back and low by stretching out his neck and raising his head to the horizontal, and trots forward with mouth open, uttering short, guttural grunts. He also regularly uses the threat gesture to keep his harem together, or to bring back a hind that may have strayed away some hundred metres. He employs the same threat to round up any loose hinds. In both cases he leaves his harem, the members of which are generally content to simply raise their heads and watch the proceedings, and trots out to the female or females to be rounded up. Going beyond them, he herds them back, and a few steps are usually sufficient to set them in motion.

But the stag does not always succeed in restraining a hind that is seeking to break away. Within the harem there may be a dominant hind which, in the hurly-burly of the rut, has been displaced far from her home range. She can sometimes dictate where she and her family will go, in spite of the stag. During one rut I witnessed such a dominant hind commence the trek back to her home range, and though the master stag tried to head her off, she outfaced him easily, by running uphill to return to familiar ground, and the rest of the harem followed behind her. He lost the lot.

Hinds can outrun the heavier stags, especially uphill. A pursuing stag does not waste energy unnecessarily. He seems to know when it is no longer worth running further, and will quickly give up. He is more likely to abandon the chase where stags are holding hinds within about 300 metres of each other, where he would encroach on an adjoining territory.

The territory exclusive to a rutting stag is a moveable one. It surrounds the harem, and moves when the hinds move. Hinds change feeding grounds, as for example when they leave the higher ground in the evening and move downhill to the green grass by stream margins, known in the Kerry mountains as *inches*. As they move, the holder takes up the rear, and follows at the same pace as the hinds, occasionally roaring.

Even so, master stags have traditional rutting stands, and a stag can be seen to return on successive years to the same stand, though he may be absent for a year, and then come back the next. There seems to be a definite effort made by a master stag to hold his hinds on one of the more level benches, where he can run more easily, and survey the surrounding country from an adjacent rocky outcrop. The interaction of sika and red deer males on the same rutting stands is complex. The sika buck appears to be more territorial, and I have several times observed a buck drive off a stag from the bench he occupied, and which the sika obviously considered to be his own.

Another common activity by the stag during the rut is threshing. There are various kinds, with different levels of intensity. A stag will attack a furze bush, a tussock of purple moor-grass, or a clump of bracken, and swiftly demolish it, vigorously swiping his antlers from side to side or back and forth, and frequently carrying off some of the vegetation on them. If threshing is intense, the stag may become sexually aroused, and after a prolonged bout of threshing and roaring, often urinates on the spot. A variation on this type of behaviour is goring the ground with his antlers, particularly his brow tines, which he digs in and then lunges savagely upwards, tossing earth and vegetation over his head. Generally, goring the ground is a more intense activity, and the stag is visibly more aroused than in simple threshing. Indeed he may even make sudden lunges and rushes forward as if fighting an imaginary foe, and then finish with a bout of prolonged roaring.

The stag may also attack a small tree, continuing to thresh it for about twenty minutes, sometimes with a vigour equal to a full stag fight. A stag will regularly thresh the same tree, especially a willow, returning again and again to do battle with a particular branch, strip the bark, and lick the exposed fresh sap. Having demolished a large furze bush, he goes for the stumps, flaying the bark with his antlers, and licking the sap. He then rubs the side of his face against the stump, anointing it with the resinous fluid from his preborital gland, licking yet again. Feral goats in the park also break furze with their horns and lick the sap.

Rubbing the antlers, face, forehead, cheeks, eyes and neck against stripped branches is common to many stags, including those that do not hold a harem. One of the latter regularly returned to an old post of a fenced-off plot, which he repeatedly abraded for about 15 minutes with his antlers, and then proceeded to lick as if bark had been exposed, though there was, of course, no sap whatsoever. A solitary mountain ash below Stompacoumeen was so frequently used by stags for this purpose, that its roots were laid bare with the churning up of the ground at its base, and the tree itself was almost entirely debarked from the constant chafing of antlers. This type of behaviour also takes place against any isolated wooden post left erect on the bare mountain-side. In the lowlands, antlers are rubbed against the trunks of mature trees, as for example in some of the patches of woodland in Bunrower.

The stag while threshing often sprays as well, producing a powerful and sustained jet of urine which he directs forward between his front legs and, by lowering and twisting his head, he covers his face, throat and belly in the spray. He does this in the vicinity of the harem and normally the hinds take little notice. Threshing and spraying are considered to be a means of marking territory[2].

Stags wallowing during the rut do so alone. Just as some master stags return to the same rutting stand year after year, likewise some repeatedly use traditional wallowing pools. A master stag deliberately herds his harem towards the wallow, which he then proceeds to use, himself. He generally begins by smelling carefully all around, and then smelling the wallow. He often enlarges the hollow by pawing at the ground with his forefoot, at the same time lowering his head, nose close to the ground, antlers thrust forward and back arched. He also uses his antlers to dig out the wet peat and to gore the earth, showering the ground all around him with peat slurry. He then lies down in the muck and starts to roll, turning on his side with legs outstretched, and sometimes raking his antlers vigorously across the wet surface. A stag will wallow right up to his eyes, throwing the mud over his back with his antlers and endeavouring to coat back and flank with wet peat. He may then stand up, start pawing again, and then lie down once more, but on his other side, and repeat the process all over again. But there are also quiet periods during the wallow, and as the rut progresses and the master stag tires, sometimes he can be seen in the wallow, dozing off to sleep for a few brief moments.

As the wallowing continues, the stag becomes more and more agitated and excited. After covering himself in black muck, he again stands inside the wallow, pawing vigorously and urinating repeatedly into the pool. When finished, he climbs out and stands to one side, energetically shaking himself in a cascade of water droplets. Next he roars loudly several times, first uphill, then downhill. A stag emerging from a wallow is covered from head to hoof in glistening, black peat, and as he returns to the harem, his gait may change, as he adopts a high stepping, prancing walk, and roars repeatedly. A stag so aroused is a dangerous animal, and in my experience may advance towards a human intruder, roaring at him and warning him off. It is best to give him all the space that he needs.

Hinds also wallow during the rut, but their activity is nothing like that of the stag. It looks similar to the roll around in the wet peat in the spring and summer.

Lone stags also wallow, visiting the various pools as they travel the hillsides. In one exceptional instance during the 1990 rut, a loose association of seven young stags approached a wallow together, and then stood around, each waiting his turn, as one after another wallowed, then threshed the vegetation, roared, and went on.

Whether he be a master or a young stag, there is always a marked attempt to cover the antlers in the wet peat, and sometimes he will visit a wallow and merely coat his antlers and move off again.

The best known and most spectacular rutting activity is roaring. This varies in intensity and duration and between individuals. Different roars mean different things. While holding hinds, a master stag lies up a considerable amount of the time, and utters a single roar at intervals, which vary at first from five to ten minutes, but can lengthen to half an hour as the stag tires. These may be described as *holding roars*. They advertise his presence and presumably his possession of hinds. They also locate any loose stags travelling about the mountain in search of hinds, since any roar is usually answered by any other stag within earshot. Hours may pass like this, with the holder lying up in an advantageous position on a slope above his harem, alert and watchful. The holding roar is often enough to start off other master stags with an answering holding roar, and sometimes bouts of roaring ensue. Generally about midday, and for an hour or so before and after it, the frequency of roaring decreases and there may be some hours of comparative quiet on the hills. Nevertheless, there are days in every rut of exceptional roaring, when it continues unabated.

When loose stags are on the move, in early morning and at dusk, there are prolonged bouts of roaring throughout the hills and valleys. A holder may roar as often as six times per minute, or a roar every 10–12 seconds. After a minute or two there is a lull and then he starts again. But throughout the last half hour or so of late evening, as light is failing, the sound can be almost continuous, as six or seven masters stand on their rutting grounds and bellow, so that between them there is a roar about every two seconds. The sound, echoing in the stillness of a high mountain coum, has a wonderful ring of wildness and freedom about it. To experience it on a calm, crisp October evening, when a raven's wing-beats are audible in the stillness, is one of the most thrilling experiences in all of Ireland's wild nature. The stags quieten down as dusk settles into night, but roaring goes on day and night. I was able to verify this while spending entire nights on the open mountain. On three different years I heard roaring in every hour of darkness.

When roaring has continued for some time, it sometimes stimulates a yearling male to join in. His efforts produce a shorter, high pitched, fragmented sound, and it is as if the youngster's voice had not yet broken. Continuous roaring also attracts the attention of calves. On a few occasions I have observed a calf look at a bellowing stag and then begin to call out with a peculiar shrill bark each time the stag roared. This was repeated many times and brought the calf's mother running hurriedly to its side.

A deerwatcher can distinguish the roars of some individual stags after two or three weeks, and thus locate them by ear as they move about the hills. Also, as the rut progresses, roaring becomes hoarser, and now the holding roar sounds tired. It is feebler and more drawn out, even somewhat wailing, and lacks its original immediacy and authority. Some master stags that have become very tired regularly doze off between holding roars. But it would be wrong to assume that they are no longer alert. In the 1980 rut, towards the end of the third week of October, I stalked in close to such a stag so as to photograph him. As he roared I was able to see his wildly rolling eye through the camera lens, and I could actually see the gleam of recognition in it as, in mid-roar, he heard the camera shutter. He was up and away even before the roar had died in his throat. Such speed of reaction is characteristic of all rutting stags, even tired ones.

During the rut, sometimes a stag will stop, raise his head, open his mouth in the roaring position, but he does not roar. Instead he flares back his upper lip, and with mouth slightly open, slowly bobs his head up and down, at the same time swivelling it from side to side. A stag may do this almost anywhere, and holders do it regularly. It has been described in the literature as *flehmen*, and according to one authority[3], the stag is testing the air for the scent of a hind in oestrous by exposing structures on the inside of his upper lip, the Jacobsen's pits, which are specialised, highly sensitive organs of smell.

Life continues much as normal for hinds, calves and followers throughout the rut. Hinds graze as usual, taking apparently little notice of the roaring and rutting stag trotting about them. Likewise they lie up and chew the cud, at the same times and for the same periods. Calves, now three to three and a half months old, still suckle vigorously, even as the holder bellows near by. However, a very late calf – and one or two of these may be seen at each rut – can be obviously intimidated by the mere presence of a master stag. The size difference between the two is immense. The calf may be only a few weeks old and white spotted; whereas the master stag may be eight times bigger, and perhaps twice the size of a hind, especially if he is a lowland stag herding hill hinds. In one such instance, when the master stag roared, the young calf would run to hide itself at the side of its mother farthest from the stag, and peer out apprehensively from underneath her neck at the holder's approach. Perhaps also a calf can be displaced in the bustle and noise of the rut. In the last week of October in the 1991 rut in the lowlands, a solitary late calf of four to six weeks old appeared on the lake shore, near the mouth of the River Flesk. It was so thin that its sides seemed to touch each other. Yet it could run quickly into the alder woods, but it could hardly have survived.

As October advances, the weather is getting colder, the days shorter, and there is a tendency for the hinds to drift towards the greens along the river inches, especially when the mountain grasses begin to wither. The stag in possession will follow and herd them wherever they go, and the change in weather does not dampen his ardour. If anything the rut may even intensify with a drop in temperature, and crisp mornings in late October are notorious for prolonged and loud roaring, with the stag's breath condensing into visible clouds in the frosty air. More frequently in Killarney it is a mixture of rain and wind, with blustery showers of hail, and some snow dusting the higher summits. Cold weather was a feature of part of the 1981 rut. A stag rutted and roared on the summit of Torc, at an altitude of 550 metres, on ground frozen rock hard. Again, during the 1990 rut, on 8 October, a stag herded five hinds and a calf at over 600 metres on the north facing slopes of Mangerton, which were frozen hard and held considerable tracts of black ice.

Likewise, rutting and roaring continues even in the heaviest of rain and the strongest of winds. Out of the few thousands of instances of roaring which I have observed, some of the most memorable have been in heavy rain and gales. The colours of rocks and vegetation then take on a luminous intensity in the clinging wetness characteristic of the Kerry mountains, when the sight of a roaring stag, of his head of antlers, surge of strength and sheer presence can be breathtakingly magnificent.

The rut in the lowlands has a different character. The quivering roars of a stag, usually hidden in damp alder woods, have a distinct timbre as a half-echo sounds through the trees. Wallowing in the lowlands occurs deep within these woods, or along the lakeshore, where the stag is more often heard than seen. A freshly used lowland wallow reeks with the odour of rutting in the stillness of the woodland floor; in the mountains the wind quickly dissipates such scent. Some October rutting days in the lowland woods can be mild and sunny, with spectacular views along the lake's limestone shoreline. And the lowland rut can also be glorious in rain and high winds. Then the roaring of the stags mingles with and is lost in the noise of the gale as it rushes through windward trees and swishes through russet bracken and is muffled by the constant sounds of white-capped waves running across the lake's black surface and by the rustle of wind-scattered leaves, red, yellow and amber. If the evening clears, the voices of the stags will carry far across the lake, as rainbows grow and vanish against the hills.

Rutting stags drink frequently, and they also graze, though their food intake has dropped drastically. A holder, while grazing or drinking, is less wary than the hinds; it is the hinds which are on the alert and give the alarm-bark. However, the stag in possession is, night and day, ever watchful for other stags seeking to take his harem.

Many loose stags are travelling the hills and outnumber the holders. They are constantly on the look-out for a stray hind to capture and hold. An older stag, past his prime, either resorts to an old rutting ground or a traditional stag wintering area, where he may still succeed in holding just one hind.

Stags of over two years old, but not yet sufficiently mature to become holders, engage in roaring bouts to test the strength and condition of a stag in possession. They also release aggression by fighting a dead tree branch or bush, in an apparently imaginary battle. One such animal, which had succeeded in herding a few hinds in November after the main rut was over, had a typical engagement with a dead tree branch at a stream's outwash. He attacked the branch viciously, with head down and antlers presented as he would have in a stag fight. The slender branch, still supple, sprang back towards him, but this only excited him to even greater fury. The "fight" lasted 10 minutes. During one rut I watched, on the open mountain, a solitary mature-looking stag act out an imaginary fight all on his own. First he stopped and carefully smelled around a rock outcrop which contained some heather and dwarf furze, perhaps where another stag had lain. He then suddenly lowered his head and rushed forward, back arched, and lunged upwards with his antlers, attacking an imaginary foe with pushing movements, and wheeling and turning with a speed and ferocity worthy of any real stag fight. He stopped after a few minutes and loped away over the hills.

A potential challenger, increasingly secure in his own feeling of strength and condition and impelled by the urgency of the rutting instinct, will stop in his tracks when he hears a holding roar. If the source is out of sight and not in his direction of travel, he will immediately change course, making straight for the unseen holder. As he approaches the stag in possession, he has several options. He can work up a challenge; he can withdraw; or he can pass by, skirting the holder and his harem. The ways in which he passes by in the Killarney mountains are interesting. If the master stag walks out deliberately, 100 metres or so from his harem, roaring repeatedly, the loose stag may go beyond that master stag, giving him a wide berth, but roaring vigorously himself just the same. Once he has passed by, the master stag usually threshes the ground and vegetation, and returns to his harem, still roaring. Alternatively, the loose stag may not roar at all, but detour around with his head lowered, and with every appearance of meekness and submission. Such submissive circumvention is not common on the open mountain slopes, where there is sufficient space to allow of token defiance. It is more frequent on broken ground, especially between long parallel ribs of rock outcrop, as for example on the steep east side of the Stompacoumeen ridge, where a loose stag is forced closer to the holder whilst passing by.

Sooner or later the master stag will be challenged, either by another master or by a younger stag seeking to take possession of the hinds. When this happens, the pattern of roaring is noticeably different. Initially, challenging roars increase in frequency and intensity but are not always answered by the holder. A master stag on Torc that held five hinds replied repeatedly to the roars of another holder, but did not answer a young stag who was also near by, and roaring. Somehow the young stag's voice seemed to lack authority, and perhaps the holder sensed this.

A challenging stag will roar every four or five seconds. A defending holder, as he watches his rival approach, sometimes starts with an explosive "cough-roar", or "bark-roar", short and sharp. If he is strong and vigorous, he can then roar every one or two seconds for the first half minute or so – about 16 to 18 roars in quick succession. Thereafter he slows down a little. The challenger, if serious, also roars louder and more frequently; one challenger roared eight times in 10 seconds, and followed this up with 49 roars in six minutes. Research in Scotland[1] has shown that rival stags can judge each other's condition and fitness by such vocal contests.

If the challenger still means business, the roaring bouts end with the master stag walking out to the challenger, and the rivals meeting with antlers lowered. After a short rush, antlers are locked and a stag fight begins. More usually, however, both stags commence a parallel walk, about 10 to 20 metres apart, with each sizing up his opponent. The value of this ritual is obvious: either animal may swiftly pull out at any time and flee, thereby avoiding a costly fight. The parallel walk has many variations. In the Killarney hills sometimes it is very short, of no more than five or six paces before a fight, or withdrawal, though at least two such rituals that I witnessed lasted for 15–20 minutes. It is also generally uphill, though sometimes the animals meander about on the more level benches. Both stags slowly and deliberately pace forward, either in a circle, or figure of eight, or even a rough square. Roaring continues during the walk and sometimes one contestant will break off and thresh the ground vigorously. This is not the usual threshing of vegetation, but a vicious goring of the ground with the brow tines, and ends with savage upward thrusts of the antlers, sending vegetation and sods flying in the air. Such threshing is brief; the pacing, parallel to each other, then resumes. Even after a prolonged parallel walk there may still be no fight, the challenger withdrawing and running off, the holding stag returning to his harem, mounting a hillock and roaring. Such assessment of strength and condition is important, as a stag's ultimate breeding success depends on his fighting ability. Unless he can fight successfully, he will not gain access to a harem and may not breed at all, unless he has the chance of picking up a stray hind at the end of the rut.

Consequently, contrary to some popular descriptions, fights are common, especially from about the second week in October, when the master stags are beginning to tire. When a fight is about to occur, there is a definite invitation to combat. One stag lowers and slightly turns his head, presenting his antlers to the other. This may not be accepted, of course, and the would-be opponent withdraws. Or it may appear at first that it will be accepted, but then fizzle out. In one parallel walk on Ferta, both stags presented antlers to each other but then stood for some moments before withdrawing and recommencing the walk. After a few minutes both again presented antlers, the tips about a metre apart and quivering. But again they withdrew and recommenced the walking and roaring. Eventually the downhill stag retreated, and it was over.

If the challenge is accepted, then both lower their heads and, with a sudden rush, antlers are locked and a stag fight is in progress. It is a trial of strength. The animals immediately commence pushing and, as gravity is an important factor, the invitation to fight almost always comes from the protagonist higher up on a slope. In a prolonged contest, both stags' backs are arched, heads held low, almost to the ground, and the vigorous pushing soon becomes a series of wheeling turns, as the animal up-slope attempts to push the other down, at the same time twisting his antlers, and trying to throw his opponent on his side. Should he succeed, he will endeavour to gore him in the flank. However, the stag down-slope usually can swiftly parry this thrust by wheeling around, and letting his opponent's momentum carry him downhill, so that now the positions are reversed, and so the wheeling goes on. A stag's strength is such that he can, in a furious rush and with a savage upward lunge of his head and antlers, momentarily lift his opponent off the ground.

Sometimes a fight which has begun on level open ground progresses into rough, rocky terrain, and this demands nimble footwork and side stepping, as the animals push and turn amidst the boulders. But many stag fights start and finish on steep slopes among rock outcrops, where it would seem almost impossible for the contestants to hold their footing. On one exceptional occasion, on 17 October when the rut was well advanced, I witnessed four stag fights, between seven individual stags – one fighting twice – among the rocks and steep broken ground of Stompacoumeen, all within the space of a quarter of an hour. Two of the contests were swiftly over, the third lasted about two minutes, and the fourth perhaps four minutes. Though the fight itself may sometimes be out of sight, the clash of antlers is distinctly audible, up to almost a kilometre away on a calm day,

While fighting, after some minutes the opponents may break away and confront each other, standing a few metres apart, still with heads lowered and antlers presented. Then they dash together again, lock antlers, pushing and wheeling as before, each repeatedly using the sudden twist to try and throw his opponent. As the antlers are engaged, it is the angle between the strong brow tine and the main antler beam which catches and takes the strain as the stag endeavours to overthrow his rival. This is one of the strongest and thickest parts of the antler. On a sika buck's antler there is an obvious raised bony ridge in the angle between brow tine and beam which reinforces this angle, and sika bucks do fight with great vigour and aggressiveness. Sometimes so intense is a sika fight that it is possible to approach quite closely, especially at dusk. Notwithstanding, all such battles are inherently dangerous and are best viewed from a safe distance.

The importance of antler size in deciding fights is sometimes overemphasised. It is body size, weight and condition which are important, and a fresh stag with smaller antlers and fewer points can on occasion defeat a bigger stag with larger antlers, who is tired and weakened from rutting. I have observed this in the Killarney hills on several occasions. On 17 October 1992, a large lowland stag – there was no doubt about this because he was ear-tagged – that had come up for the rut was routed by a smaller hill stag.

To witness the strength and fury of a prolonged stag fight, close up, is a relatively rare privilege. Most contests that I have seen were brief. After a few skirmishes and pushes the weaker animal withdrew and fled, sometimes pursued by the victor for about 30 or 40 metres. In one instance, on the slopes of Cloughfune, after a swift fight in which the challenger won, the loser ran downhill and jumped straight into a wallow, reduced to bouts of roaring as he threw wet peat over his back with his antlers. Occasionally a combat is prolonged. The longest fight which I have witnessed lasted about 15 minutes, on the open ground south of Cores. At the end the loser had been seriously wounded in the face. He quickly withdrew, shaking his head vigorously.

Injury during a stag fight is common, and in Scotland it was found that about a quarter of rutting stags suffered some injury during the rut[5]. If the same rate of injury were to apply to Kerry, then, since the period over which a stag can successfully rut is effectively about four to six years, it is probable that almost every master stag will suffer injury at some time. Certainly, in the Killarney hills, it is common to see animals with broken antlers, facial wounds and lame forelegs, towards the end of the rut and afterwards. Wounds are mostly to the head: eye and nose injuries, and also split ears, are common.

A master stag can suffer injury but can still continue to hold hinds. A very lame lowland stag, whose left hind leg had been previously broken but had healed naturally, kept seven hinds and three calves in Prospect, during the 1992 rut. Rutting stags in the Killarney mountains with half of one antler missing have still maintained a harem well into the third week in October. I once observed a master stag with a broken antler herding up to 10 hinds. This, however, was exceptional and probably did not last very long. Antlers which are broken off half-way up the beam do not seem to seriously inhibit the ability to keep a harem. Nevertheless, it is rare to see a stag in Killarney suc-

Plate 16   High on Torc's summit, an 8-pointer stag catches the early morning sunlight

Plate 17   Roaring: stag in full voice near Cromagloun Mountain

Plate 18   Close-up detail of roaring stag, Crinneagh area

Plate 19   The thick mane and neck is typical of a red stag in rut, at c. 600 metres on Mangerton Mountain

Plate 20   The loping trot adopted by a stag as he travels the mountains during the rut

Plate 21   One of the great stags of the 1970s: "the Cores 14-pointer", in full voice in the Crinneagh area

Plate 22   A large lowland master stag, up in the mountains for the October rut

Plate 23   The most successful of all stags in the author's experience, "Growler", during the late 1980s rut

Plate 24   Stag utilising flehmen *activity in lowland habitat, autumn*

Plate 25   Another view of the dominant stag, "Growler"

Plate 26   Another view of "the Cores 14-pointer"

Plate 27   An aroused solitary stag threshes the vegetation and sprays himself during the rut; Crinneagh area

Plate 28   A mountain stag, alert during the October rut

Plate 29   A master stag roars amidst flowering furze during the October rut

Plate 30   High on Torc, a stag travels the mountain slopes above Killarney's lake system

Plate 31   Grace and elegance: red hind on Cromagloun Mountain

Plate 32   Mountain stag on the alert during the October rut

Plate 33   A mountain stag, pacing the hills

Plate 34   A late calf hides behind its parent hind as a master stag approaches

Plate 35   Master stag holding his unusually large harem on Mangerton

Plate 36   Master stag holding typically sized harem on Torc Mountain

Plate 37   A leading dominant hind outfaces the holding master stag as she returns to her home range

Plates 38 and 39   Master stag chivvying his hinds; Crinneagh old field systems

Plate 40   Master stag muzzle-licking hind; Crinneagh old field systems

Plate 41   Invitation to fight: the uphill stag is the first to challenge; Cores Mountain area

Plate 42   Two well-matched master stags on a parallel walk; Stompacoumeen Mountain slopes

Plate 43   A stag fight on the typically difficult and rocky terrain of Stompacoumeen

Plate 44   *The stag that died in a stag fight, photographed alive during the previous year's rut*

Plate 45   *Stag, still in* rigor mortis, *killed in a stag fight; his opponent's antler point has pierced his windpipe*

Plate 46   A subdominant stag, out of focus in foreground, submissively passing a master stag; Stompacoumeen area

Plate 47   An exceptional stag during the 1980s: "the Shaky Bog 12-pointer"

Plate 48   A master stag feeds avidly during the rut in the lowland pastures

Plate 49   Typical rutting wallow on Ferta Mountain slopes

Plate 50   In heavy rain, a stag with one broken antler, the result of a stag fight, still holds hinds

Plate 51   The after-effects of the rut: a tired stag asleep in October sunshine

Plate 52   A closer view of "the Shaky Bog 12-pointer", near Cromagloun Mountain

cessfully defending hinds if one of his brow tines is broken off. One such exception, missing one brow tine, held hinds in the Davy's Fields area during the 1989 rut.

After witnessing many stag fights, I have little doubt that it is the brow tines which are most important in a fight; these are the tines which do the serious damage as a stag gores his opponent. Older stags who have lost most of their antler points, and whose antlers have developed into switch heads, so that the main beams terminate in long raking dagger points, are traditionally still regarded as the stags which "do the most damage" in a stag fight. This view, common in general shooting and stalking literature, was the excuse for shooting switches in Killarney, when lettings to visiting stalkers and shooting syndicates was the practice in the first half of the twentieth century. However, any fight that I witnessed in which a switch was involved was swiftly over, and the switch always lost. This is not surprising; at this advanced stage in his life the switch had already lost bulk, weight, general condition and fitness, and was hardly a match for his younger and stronger opponent.

There are additional dangers for stags rutting in the lowlands. One problem is caused by loose dogs that chase deer in the woods and pastures. Another hazard is carelessly dumped rubbish at woodland edges. In Ross Island, during the 1989 rut, a stag had coils of heavy black electric cable wound around his antlers, some of it falling across his back and trailing along the ground. This could only have been acquired when threshing near dumped rubbish. Another animal in the lowlands carried a bundle of rusted fencing wire on his antlers during the 1993 rut. These are problems which the mountain red deer do not have to cope with . . . yet.

While the benefits of fighting are obvious (a stag gets a chance of mating), the costs are obviously high in terms of injury and wounds. The ultimate cost is death, something which in my experience is extremely rare in Killarney. Only once in over 30 years of observation have I come across a stag actually killed during the rut. The carcass was still in *rigor mortis,* and the wounds clearly indicated that the animal had been killed in a fight. There were antler wounds on both of his flanks, and also through his throat, penetrating his windpipe. There were already signs of scavenging as ravens, grey crows and foxes had found the carcass, but I have no doubt that the injuries were from a stag fight. Scavengers rip and tear, and do not drill neat holes, particularly where there is little flesh, as on the throat; they go in first through the softest parts, at the anus and stomach. An examination of the carcass showed that the sequence must have been that the stag was antlered first on his left flank, the side on which he went down. He was then penetrated again on his exposed right side, and his windpipe punctured. I found the body at the height of the 1985 rut, on 13 October. In many ways it was a sad find, for I knew the stag well and had followed his progress through several ruts. This individual stag is illustrated both alive and dead. When I examined photographs of the same stag taken the previous year, it was evident that his left eye had already been damaged, most probably in a stag fight as well, and it is possible that he went blind in this eye from then on. This would have been a serious disadvantage in any subsequent combat, and clearly he was caught on his blind side. Nevertheless, it must have taken tremendous strength to bring down a beast such as this, which was estimated at death to weigh about 150 kilograms. This, more than anything else, brings home the energy, fury, and massive strength of fights between master stags.

Accounts of stags' antlers becoming inextricably locked in a fight, resulting in both animals dying a slow, lingering death, are a popular part of red deer literature. I know of only two such occurrences in Killarney. One is a local folk memory of a pair of interlocked antlers found on the western shoreline of Lough Leane, below Toamies Wood, many years ago. The other one occurred during the 1993 rut, when the carcasses of two stags with interlocked antlers were found in the wet alder woods, partly submerged, on the north side of Lough Leane. A pair of skeletons, with antlers interlocked, of red × sika hybrids were found in the Wicklow mountains, in 1982[6].

While a fight is in progress a third stag may take advantage and dash in, carrying off some, but rarely all, of the hinds. This opportunistic move is called *kleptogamy*, and the stag that does it is called a *kleptogamist*[7]! This manoeuvre is rarely successful for long; the opportunistic stag still has to fight to keep his new-found possessions and, in the instances that I witnessed, could hold the hinds for no more than about 10 hours before being himself dispossessed by a more powerful opponent. Since the period of heat in a hind is quite short, varying from six to 24 hours[8], it is doubtful if the kleptogamist, in the instances witnessed, ever benefited from his opportunistic move by actually mating.

All stags are constantly on the lookout for hinds in oestrous. The whole purpose of the rut, that period of intense sexual activity, is to mate. In the second and third week of October, the master stag is frequently urging hinds up from a lying position, and he then follows them in a little chase. That chase may be a prelude to mating. Frequently the chase is very short, and after 20 or 30 paces, if the hind does not stand, the stag desists, then she resumes grazing, and she gradually re-integrates with the harem. When pursuit intensifies, the stag may stretch out his neck, endeavouring to place his jaw and head on the hind's flank; again she frequently runs off. A hind that is not in oestrous, and therefore not ready to mate, will not accept a stag. Some chases are quite prolonged, and an exceptional one, which I witnessed throughout, lasted for over an hour. During that chase, both eventually flopped to the ground, exhausted. After a rest of about 10 minutes, the stag stood up and again began chivvying the hind, and the chase resumed; eventually, they ran out of sight behind a curve of hill.

Often a stag will approach an individual hind, as she is either lying up or grazing, and nuzzle and lick her face, going over her forehead, cheeks, eyes and ears with his tongue. These muzzle-licking bouts are generally short-lived. It is not all one sided: a hind may approach a stag, soliciting him. Sometimes a stag will come uphill swiftly and, reaching out his huge maned neck and with antlers lying flat along his back, touch the hind with his mouth. She may respond by rubbing her head and forehead up against his mane and neck. She also rubs her face and body along his flank.

If the hind is coming into oestrous, the stag stands close by her, paying her close attention to the exclusion of the others and roaring frequently. Roaring has been found to advance the onset of oestrus in hinds[9]. Occasionally he may herd her away, or simply follow her if she wanders off grazing, leaving the harem behind. The pair may thus remain separated from his other hinds until mating occurs. Outlying stags are aware of this, and a holder paying court to one hind may find himself surrounded by up to four other, younger, stags, all roaring, and trying to take away some of the unattended hinds. Sometimes they succeed.

Actual mating is very rarely witnessed, and is generally seen from afar. Mating can occur at any time of day, but in Scotland it was found[10] to peak at morning and evening. If a stag endeavours to mount the hind while she is not receptive, she simply kicks him off with her hind legs, and runs away. When the hind is fully receptive, she stands with hind legs slightly splayed, and the stag mounts from the rear. In one of the sequences that I witnessed, the stag made a final lunge with neck stretched straight up, face looking up at the sky, which is traditionally taken to indicate a successful mating. Then the hind ran forward as he came off behind her. I estimated the mating took about four to five seconds. The hind stayed where she stopped after the little run, and remained stationary, with back arched, for about 10 minutes. On another occasion, I counted just four seconds for the actual mating, and again the hind was pushed forward, after which she then stood stationary for perhaps five minutes. Such a stance by the hind is also taken as a sign that mating has been accomplished.

There may be several attempts before success. A stag will sometimes mount a hind a second time, immediately following the first effort. The greatest number of mountings that I have witnessed was five, in quick succession, before mating was achieved. Practically all copulations and attempted copulations in the Kerry hills have, in my experience, occurred between 10–24 October. The act was always quickly over. That swiftness is understandable in a species which would be vulnerable to predators while in the act.

The mating activities of sika deer in the mountains are similar to that of red deer. But sika are especially pugnacious, and a buck may be called on to do more than just mate, as happened in one incident I witnessed on 21 October during the 1972 rut. A large buck chased a doe in and out amongst grassy tussocks, rocks and withered ferns, uttering the high-pitched whine peculiar to sika. He was followed at a short distance by three other bucks, smaller, obviously younger, and that kept their distance from each other. The doe went uphill, and the large buck followed her, the others trailing behind. She slowed, and then stopped to graze. The large buck tried to mount her from behind, but on three occasions she quickly pulled away from him. A little chase followed and then, after she halted to graze once more, the buck again tried to mount. On the fourth occasion he was successful, and apparently full copulation occurred; again the duration was quite short, a matter of a few seconds. After this the buck and doe separated. She ran off a little and commenced to graze. But he wheeled immediately downhill, antlers lowered, and met the challenge of one of the younger bucks that was already rushing up from below, with antlers also lowered. They met head on, antlers locked low down, and began fighting. The large buck, pushing downhill, easily won, forcing the younger one backwards. A few metres of this and the younger buck gave up and wheeled away. However the fight was not over. Once more the younger buck returned and they fought again, antlers locked, heads down, twisting and pushing. As before, the larger buck with a powerful rush defeated the challenger; it was a mystery how the younger and lighter animal was able to keep his balance before that rush of strength. The large buck immediately went after another doe, and out of sight.

Although some individual stags are easy enough to recognise year after year during the rut, it would be impossible to say how many times a stag can successfully mate each year, without continuous observation, day and night, requiring special equipment and several trained observers. In one Scottish study it was found[11] that the most successful stags fathered about a dozen calves during each rut. In another study[12] the most successful stags – in this case those who had fathered five to six calves – made up less than 5% of the rutting males, and over 45% of the latter accounted for about one calf apiece. The successful mating rate is unknown for Killarney, but based on an estimated 30 to 35 dominant stags who seem to control the mountain rut, and subsequent calf counts of 90 to 120, the average may be three to four calves per stag. But, like the Scottish results, it is likely that there is considerable variation between individuals. Some of the Killarney stags in the mountains seem to keep a harem for a few days only, whereas exceptional individuals can do this for much longer. For example, one animal that regularly rutted in the Ferta area of Mangerton, and who was known as "Growler" because of his exceptionally deep, guttural roar, held hinds for at least three weeks, over three successive ruts.

It was also found in Scotland[13] that some stags went through their entire lives without ever breeding. It is something which I had long suspected from watching individual animals over many years in Killarney, but could never prove. It is an important point. Stags, both Irish and foreign, were introduced to Killarney in the nineteenth and early twentieth centuries. However, it is an open question as to whether they ever mated, particularly as they were likely to have been at a disadvantage in achieving dominance in a strange new environment.

Likewise, a female may never mate. Such an animal is referred to as a *barren* hind, and is distinct from a female which does not mate in one particular year, but "takes a rest", and which is called a *yeld* hind. A hind will apparently run yeld if she does not reach a critical weight, level of fitness and condition. This is sometimes observed at Killarney, and is easily understood when the harshness of a mountain winter, coupled with the energy drain of raising a calf on acid vegetation, is taken into account. It is not known whether all lowland hinds at Killarney breed every year, though the percentage of calves to hinds is greater in the lowlands than in the mountains. It is possible that a higher survival rate in the lowlands may be partly responsible. In any case, since there is some interchange between the mountain and lowland red deer, it is a point yet to be established in the wild, from observation of tagged animals.

The rut does not suddenly end; it peters out. In early November roaring is still occasionally heard in the hills, but it is a tired affair. A stag that held a few hinds on 3 November stood with his eyes closed and head nodding, asleep on his feet. However, by about the third week in October some of the master stags have already been ousted by challengers and, once displaced, it is interesting to note their behaviour. Master stags eat much less during the rut than in summer. Some Scottish animals were found to loose about 20% of their body weight and 80% of their fat in those short three weeks[14]. A holder ousted towards the end of his rut begins to feed avidly. One that I witnessed commenced to graze *immediately* after he had been displaced from his harem. A stag at this stage is so hungry, and grazes so eagerly, that sometimes he will even ignore the alarm-bark of a hind; something which would never happen at other times of the year. But he will still occasionally roar. Indeed a stag can lift his head from grazing and roar with the bite still in his mouth.

The younger and fresher stags, which now take possession of the hinds, will mate with any which come into late oestrous. Evidence for late oestrous is provided by the few calves with spots, and therefore about three to four weeks old, which are seen during the October rut. Their mothers must have mated in the previous January, as the normal gestation period for hinds is usually given as about 234–36 days. In the polygamous society of red deer, any hind in oestrous will be mated. The latest rutting activity that I have observed was 7 February 1981 at Cloghfune, where a stag was roaring, rounding up hinds, and attempting to mate, albeit unsuccessfully.

The season of oestrous in sika is also extended. On the one hand, those in the Killarney lowlands have been known to mate as early as late August, their calves being dropped by the following April. On the other hand, in the mountains I have witnessed a buck mating with a doe on Ferta on 1 December 1984. On 27 December 1991, I witnessed a particularly savage fight between two bucks in the lowland area of Knockreer, that matched any during the October rut, suggesting that, even then, rutting was unfinished.

There is little doubt that some young red stags, prevented from mating by masters, experience sexual frustration during and after the rut. As late as 19 December, while on an early morning lowland count with Park Ranger Peter O'Toole, I watched a young stag mounting another equally young stag from the rear, and then lunging forward, head thrown skyward, and then backing off. Sexual activity among adolescent deer is common enough, but it appeared to us that on this occasion the animal had actually ejaculated. Such activity by young red stags may yet have a sinister outcome, and lead to red × sika hybridisation, as the red population increases. The introduced sika sometimes graze side by side with the native red deer in Killarney, and a sika doe in late oestrous might be receptive to, and covered by, a young red stag. Once started, experience elsewhere has shown that hybridisation quickly spreads. This would be catastrophic for the genetic purity of our native red deer.

While the rut has effectively tailed off by the end of November, such occasional activity as lingers on is not affected by the onset of severe winter weather. Cold does not dampen a stag's ardour. I was surprised to find, after an exceptionally heavy snowfall in December 1981, a stag roaring and herding hinds in the Davy's Fields area. Half a metre or so of snow cover presented no problem to his powerful stride and long legs.

Such, however, are rare occurrences. As October draws to a close, the vast majority of the stags have finished with the rut. Likewise, the great majority of hinds have mated, and as winter is rapidly approaching, it is not unusual to come upon a stag asleep on the open hillside in the late October sunshine. It is no surprise, for being a master stag during the rut in Killarney is hard work. The running, roaring, threshing, spraying, wallowing, fighting, mating and lack of food and sleep have all taken their toll. And in a short four to six weeks, full winter will be upon the mountains.

IV

Winter

Is ann a-dubairt Caílte: "Inam," ar sé, "do dhamhaib allaidi &
d'eilltibh dul a n-innib cnoc & carrac an-osa . . ." & a-dubhuirt an laíd:
Is úar geimred; at-racht gáeth;
éirgid dam díscir dergbáeth;
  nocha te in-nocht in slíab slán,
  gé beith dam dían ac dordán.

Then Caílte spoke: "It is time," said he, "for stags and does to withdraw
to the inmost parts of hills and rocks . . ." And he spoke this poem.

"Winter is cold; the wind has risen; the fierce stark-wild stag arises; not
warm tonight is the unbroken mountain, even though the swift stag be
belling."

Irish poem, c. 1175 A.D.[1]

November is the most colourful month in the Killarney lowlands: the woodlands are a riot of russets, reds, ochres, yellows and varying tones of brown.
Often it also is a very wet month, and the saturated atmosphere lends an
intensity of colour to everything, enhancing the hues of withering leaves, and bejew-
elling each twig and blade of grass with droplets of moisture. By now, most of the
tourists have long since packed up and gone away.

   In the mountains, winter has already arrived. While November may well be a relatively mild month, in the mountains there are frequent gales and rain, sweeping
across from the south-west, west and north-west, reducing visibility to about 100
metres, and smothering the higher peaks in wet, clinging mist. Ireland's highest rainfall has been recorded in the Kerry mountains, up to 4,000 millimetres in a year[2]. Life
goes on for the red deer, and even in the heaviest rain they still graze, heads down,
with rumps to the rain and wind. Already the weather is beginning to have an effect
which will continue, and intensify, for many months to come: the exposure to pro-

longed rain and high winds uses up energy that has been stored from summer feeding. As the temperature falls and daylight decreases the red deer adjust, and activity and appetite are noticeably reduced. When winter advances and tightens its grip, the deer on the hills split up into smaller family units and overall numbers fall. After the rut, some mountain deer migrate to the lowlands, particularly to the woodland margins adjoining the lake shores. And increases in winter numbers of lowland red deer were recorded during research in the early 1980s[3]. As Dotey Donoghue, who lived in the Derrycunnihy woodlands, used to remark it the 1970s: "The deer will be coming down soon, and some will be so worn out from the rut, they will be hardly able to walk!"

Where all the red deer that leave the hills actually spend the winter is not yet fully established. Some migrate to Muckross, because animals tagged in the last few years, and observed in the mountains in October, were seen again in the Muckross area shortly after the rut and throughout the following winter. Counts of the mountain herd reveal that, in winter, numbers on average were about 30–50% of those in summer. However, the increase in numbers in Muckross in winter is smaller than the corresponding decrease in the mountains.

Amongst the wild red deer which stay in the mountains throughout the winter are some master stags. These can still be seen on the hills, often on the sheltered slopes, and sometimes occupying ledges on cliff sides, where now and again they can be seen asleep in afternoon winter sunshine.

After the rut, stags regroup into herds of varying size. It is the time for new recruits to join these bachelor groups, and younger stags that have been pushed out during the rut now seek to join the older males. From now on these troops will live apart and distinct from the maternal assemblages of hinds, calves, yearlings and two year olds. Males now re-establish a form of hierarchy, if necessary by the aggressive use of antlers, though there is no fighting as such involved, and the younger, weaker animals give way and avoid conflict. Once settled, dominance is likely to be maintained while the group remains cohesive. If it fragments and different individuals regroup, dominance will be again asserted, contested, and eventually settled.

Stags that have rutted successfully and have lost body weight now engage in intensive and prolonged feeding. In the short period from the end of October until about mid-December, the hill stags must build up fat reserves for the mountain winter. Some are naturally drawn to the lush grasses of the lowlands, especially at night-time, and can sometimes be seen grazing near roadside verges. Those stags that remain on the hill seek out whatever greens remain, and are in direct competition with the more numerous hinds, and with the many sheep that also graze the same hills within the National Park. In Scotland, as the winter advances, and cold and wind chill intensifies, hill stags were found to select locations for shelter as well as for food[4].

Some hinds and their calves migrate to the lowland, but the majority do not bother to do so and remain on the mountains. In Scotland it was found that they concentrate on the areas with the most nutritious forage[5]. In November hinds, which do not of course suffer the energy drain that the rut imposes on stags, probably attain peak condition, fat and sleek from summer grazing. Poachers well know this quality of condition, and towards the end of October or early November, it is the young hinds which they select. On the 28 October 1981 in the mountains of the National

Park a hind was found shot and *gralloched* (gutted), to use the Scottish term – in Kerry the word *paunched* is the normal expression that is used.

Hinds are adept at searching out food, as for example standing on their hind legs and reaching up for the dark green leaves of holly trees, which can be found up to about 250 metres in a few places. Red deer also eat dwarf furze, which, with heather, can be an important source of greens throughout the winter, as the mountain grasses are now withered and straw-like, the light fawn *fionaun* of the mountain winter. Three-month-old calves have no difficulty in eating furze. They neatly nibble away the yellow blossom and, by November, when they are about five months old, can nip off and eat the furze tips, despite the prickles.

Late-born calves, six to eight weeks old now, face into the coming winter at an obvious disadvantage. Inevitably some deer will die, and these late calves will be at high risk. Though winter mortality in red deer in Killarney has been poorly documented until recently, and this is dealt with in more detail in Appendix 2, the strain imposed by the rut and the onset of winter must also take its toll on adult males, both red and sika.

November in the mountains can also be quite beautiful: the sight of golden plover backlit by low angled evening sunshine amongst the rich ochres and red-browns of the upland sedges; or a short-eared owl crouching amongst withered grass, perfectly camouflaged except for its large yellow eyes and the movement of its head. The mellow light of late autumn evenings, flooding across the hills, can give to the mountains a sparkling of colours so exquisite as to be almost unreal. It highlights the deer as they graze and occasionally shake off the raindrops which gather like silver globules on their backs.

Novembers can also be punishingly harsh and cold. In 1981, Mangerton was covered by early snow before the rut had finished, and by the 16 October the summit of Torc was frozen iron hard. Mangerton was again under snow on the 10 October 1987. While such years are infrequent, the importance for the deer is that they do occur. Snowfall is more likely to be a feature of full winter, which is now virtually upon the mountains.

December, when daylight hours are shortest, can be a month of great contrasts in Killarney, contrasts both between lowland and mountain, and also between climate in different years. Decembers can be mild in the lowlands. Spindle trees flower early in the month, within the sheltered limestone cliffs around the lake shores, and in mild, damp and muggy weather, it is not unusual to find some rhododendrons in flower. Lowland red deer have the problems of avoiding human disturbance and persecution, and of avoiding being killed by vehicles on the roads at night.

The deer feed openly on the lowland pastures of the National Park, especially at night, and are a regular sight to early morning joggers and walkers in the Knockreer area. As the animals graze on the fields adjacent to woodland and lake edges, the young stags chase each other in circles through wet lush grasses. Such chases quickly end and feeding is resumed; they are more akin to play than to aggression. This activity can sometimes extend to play fights. Just inside the woodland edge there is a clash of antlers, and then the stags come into view. Young stags in their first or second antlers, with heads lowered and antlers locked, stand there but without the vigorous pushing, heaving, or twisting of a rut-style stag fight. There may even be a short "half roar", which is reminiscent of the typical "half roar" one hears in late July or early August from within the large aggregations of hill deer. Pugnacity is by no means confined to the males, and is often seen amongst the hinds, both mature and young. When a young hind repeatedly chases off a calf (sometimes the only one in the group), the latter can evade a kick by circling around to the other side of the feeding group. At times a hind can lash out quite savagely with both forelegs, and a calf has to be alert and swift to avoid this. Also there is contention amongst the mature hinds, which chase off one another, tilting their heads upwards with throat presented, or run after each other, the aggressor trying to place her chin on the rump of the retreating animal. This no longer appears like play, but has the urgency and seriousness of genuine aggression.

Though well used to man, nevertheless, as morning progresses and more people use the lowland areas of the park, the deer retreat to the concealment of woodland, where they can lie up and cud without interruption. At this time of year, stags can be seen at the woodland edge busily eating ivy from tree trunks, reaching up as high as possible and biting off the leaves with quick, tremulous movements of their mouths. Likewise, a mature hind will reach up to pull down the trailing twigs of a holly tree, which she jerks off with a toss and twist of her head, and proceeds to eat. Once in a while a hind has to use her full height, standing on her back legs and then stretching her long neck and tilting her head to its utmost, to reach the inviting evergreens. Deer also graze around fallen trees and seem to relish the fungi which grow there in profusion. The animals then lie up at the woodland edge, quietly cudding, tolerant of cock pheasants, when they happen to feed and walk amongst them. Now and again the observer may be lucky enough to get a sighting of some of the largest of the lowland stags. These magnificent beasts, heavy from the richness of feeding and with correspondingly massive antlers of up to 20 points, are very secretive, and as they frequent the deep recesses of the woodlands, are difficult to stalk and photograph.

December in the mountains is in startling contrast. The difference is never so obvious as now, and the disparity in size between lowland and mountain calves is especially striking. A lowland calf of six months can appear twice the size of a mountain calf of similar age. Temperatures in the mountains are much lower, and wind-chill is greatly enhanced. Almost without ceasing, there is the whining moan of wind and the sounds of its rushing over the mountainsides and summits. Wind in the Kerry mountains is a factor which must influence red deer dispersal and survival. In some years hard frosts also descend with a cold snap, and then the boglands are iced up, and icicles grow where erosion channels constantly drip moisture. The cold and the constant exposure to wind persistently sap energy from the deer. And in some years additionally, there can be snowfall: not merely the annual snow which mantles the higher summits, but heavy falls, which cover the lower hillsides and drift in the valley bottoms.

Such heavy snow fell in the second week in December in 1981. The winds had been high, as was usual, and much of the powder snow was blown off the exposed ridges and dumped on the valley floors. The depth of snow on the Crinneagh Flats, at an altitude of about 200 metres, was some 60 centimetres, whereas at 400 metres, on Cores Mountain, it was only about 30 centimetres. Both areas are winter habitat for the mountain red deer. Practically all water movement had stopped, with every pool frozen, and only the swiftest rivulets still ran through deep snow banks.

In these conditions, it was enlightening to compare the difference in movement between the native red deer and the introduced Japanese sika. The sika maintained their usual bounding gait, ploughing through the drifts with spurts of powder snow cascading upwards at each bound. It was heavy going, and they tired visibly. In contrast, the greater height and longer legs of the red deer enabled them to move with less effort, so that they had little difficulty in going uphill to the exposed ridges, where high winds had swept clear some of the taller vegetation. The importance of tall vegetation, such as stands of old heather and dwarf furze, is all too obvious in such conditions, providing accessible food and greens for the deer. As the animals crossed over the higher ridges, the morning sunshine reddened their coats as they moved from shadow into sunlight, affording a glorious sight against the background of snow-covered hills, a sight rare enough in Killarney, but an exquisitely beautiful one.

Strong calves are now six months old, have already put on considerable growth and display the prancing, high-stepping gait, reminiscent of that described of a stag at rut. But they are still young animals, inexperienced, and the mother-offspring relationship is all important, and crucial to the calf's survival, especially in snow. It is the older, experienced and dominant hinds which lead the way in heavy snow, seeking out where tall vegetation protrudes or leading the family group uphill to where vegetation has been exposed on windswept ridges. In my experience, a calf's response to the first snowfall of winter is one of confusion. It seems uncertain where to go, and if there is winter sunshine, it appears to be dazzled by the snow's brilliance. This sense of confusion is quickly brushed aside by the parent hind's purposeful movement and leadership, which the calf will immediately follow. A calf that had lost its mother would now be in trouble.

These mountain-bred deer on the Killarney hills, both red and the sika, are totally wild animals, without any supplementary feeding, and have adapted to cope with difficult habitats and weather conditions. The native red deer have occupied these mountains for many centuries and, because they are larger and have longer legs than sika, can not only cope better with snow but can also cross swollen mountain streams more easily. Mobility is the key. Those long, slender legs enable them to ascend and to exploit heather and dwarf furze on the higher, drier ridges, or to descend to the more accessible vegetation of the lower slopes and sheltered valleys.

In sharp contrast are the hill sheep which also graze the mountains in Killarney National Park. Selectively bred over many centuries to have shorter legs for easier rounding-up, the sheep are a pitiful sight in a heavy snowfall. They just stand there, unable to move, or flounder about, and are sometimes buried in snowdrifts. Left to themselves, the wild deer have adapted well to the mountain environment, and although not as well insulated as the thicker-coated sheep, they are nevertheless more successful in heavy snow. In south-west Cork, 70,000 ewes were alleged to have died on the mountains during the winter of 1986[6]! No significant mortality of the red deer was then recorded, nor in the exceptional heavy snows of 1947.

Heavy snowfalls extending down to about 200 metres in the Killarney mountains are uncommon and are scarcely mentioned in meteorological statistics, which are primarily compiled from the lowlands. But such heavy falls occur and can be very pertinent to the wild red deer. Even though such snow cover on the lower slopes does not last for more than three to four days, finding food and staying alive for that three to four days can be a crucial test for the mountain red deer.

There is other wildlife in the mountain winter. A succession of hard frosts frequently coincides with the arrival of flocks of redwings and fieldfares, which feast on the bright red berries of holly and late-fruiting mountain ash. In some years there is an exceptionally heavy crop, and then these flocks are followed by hen harriers, sparrowhawks and kestrels.

This is a prime time for poachers, particularly in the weeks leading up to Christmas. A succulent six-month-old calf is a particularly desirable quarry. I once witnessed and photographed poachers in action near the National Park, on the 6 December 1980. The chosen animal was a young sika and the poachers obviously knew exactly what they wanted and where to get it.

During the Christmas holidays there is a marked increase in human activity in the mountains, as both locals and visitors take the opportunity to walk on the hills. The movement of people disturbs deer, but if walkers keep to well-defined pathways, much disturbance can be minimised. A more serious problem is caused by loose dogs chasing deer. For many years it was a custom, now discouraged, for those walking off their Christmas dinner to bring unleashed dogs with them into the mountains of the National Park, which resulted in the dogs pursuing deer, sometimes for kilometres. And these dogs, many of them local, having once sampled deer hunting, subsequently returned in small groups on their own.

As January advances, the increase in daylight becomes noticeable, but temperatures in the mountain remain low, and winter tightens its grip. Some of the male calves already show signs of their pedicles sprouting. It is considered that in general male calves in the lowlands can sprout them up to a year ahead of those in the mountains. Pedicles of precocious lowland calves were already developing as far back as November, but on the mountain most of the young males do not grow them until they are already yearlings, and, as already discussed, some only produce them in September and October, when they are about 14 to 15 months old. However, in a few instances pedicles may also develop early on the mountain and late in the lowland. There was no sign of them on a male calf which was killed on the roadside by Castlerosse, in the lowlands, on the 25 January 1986.

When pedicles are first grown, they are taller and thinner than on older animals. As a young stag's first antlers sprout, there is no division apparent between pedicle and beam. Together they form one continuous, velvet-covered spike. First antlers vary a great deal. On the lowlands some are curved and long, up to 40–50 centimetres; on the mountains they are not even half that length.

All calves are still under the leadership and control of parent hinds. From now on, as the harshness of the mountain winter increases, lactation is important enough to be vital to the calf's survival. Nevertheless, it may cease at this crucial time if the mother is pregnant. Her reserves are diverted to the growing foetus and her body must also prepare for the heavy burden of lactation which will recommence when her new calf is born. On the mountain not all hinds conceive each year, and a hind which is not pregnant can continue to produce milk until the following summer. This greatly enhances the chances of her calf's surviving its first winter.

In January the hills take on their full winter appearance with the mountain grasses rain-washed, withered and deficient in nutrients. The deer concentrate on what greens there are: on the short, closely cropped mixture of heather and dwarf furze which grows up to about 600 metres, but especially on the bents and fescues, the sweet grasses which grow on the inches by the streams, and on hillside *flushes*. The flushes, where mineral-rich waters well up from the hillside, are obvious from afar as green patches, especially in winter, and are locally called *pairceens* (little fields). Grazing is heavily concentrated on such greens, and red deer here face greatest competition from sheep and sika. Mosses, lichens and the unpalatable mat-grass are also eaten, and the small pockets of mixed woodland, commonly used for shelter, are subjected to bark stripping.

The signs of bark stripping by deer are diagnostic. Being ruminants, deer have no upper *incisors* (front teeth), having instead a hard, rough pad on the palate, called the *maxillary pad*, against which the lower incisors are pressed to crop vegetation. Deer use their lower incisors to cut into the bark and then tear it off with a smart upward jerk of the head. As a result the lower end of the strip is neatly cut, whereas the upper part is torn and tapers off. Corresponding marks are left on the tree. Younger trunks and thinner branches are the most heavily attacked, older tree-trunks being too rough and too wide for their mouths. Other ruminants, sheep and feral goats, occupying the same range as the deer, also take bark, and in a similar manner. From observations over many winters, willow, birch, holly and hazel seem to be preferred, but it is not so much a question of preference as what is available, and any medium sized tree or branch within reach of the deer, or blown down by the wind will have some signs of stripping. Inevitably, some trees are ring-barked, and these are doomed to die.

By about mid-January the worst of the winter sets in. Snow comes again. The red deer are, of course, able to cope with it and, in any case, it rarely lies for long on the lower hills. More frequent, and possibly more telling on the deer, are the hard frosts of January. If the bogland is frozen solid, this can force the deer up on to the ridges (although not the summits), where heather and the dwarf furze, with some mosses and lichens, are accessible. And there is always the wind, shrieking over the ridge tops, whistling and moaning through the valley bottoms and coums and sapping away the body heat and energy of the deer. The weather statistics do not reflect the importance of the wind factor in the mountains, but it is a very real one, which can kill.

The red deer, particularly stags, seek shelter. On the lower slopes where furze grows taller, it provides not only important nourishment and greens, but also cover for red and sika alike. Deep within these expanses of furze are the pathways and runways of deer, branching and criss-crossing, and revealing where the animals go both for forage and shelter.

Some older stags are living secretly, mostly alone, although, as in summer (Chapter 2), a few form a special association with a younger stag, which seems to act as kind of attendant and sentry. If danger threatens, the old stag will drive out the younger one, which then serves, perhaps unwittingly, as a decoy, while the old one lies low. I once observed such an incident above Tower Woods at an altitude of 200–250 metres. Millais[7] knew about these associations, and referred to the younger stag as the older animal's "squire", stating that if the older stag was shot, the squire would often loiter around and refuse to go away.

The high summits over 700 metres are now deserted and are frequently frozen over, with nothing to offer the deer. Aspect, as well altitude, is important. The animals concentrate on the lower slopes facing south and south-west, which are first to thaw and which get whatever low sunshine there is. Deer avoid slopes which face north and north-east, where it is colder and snow and frost linger longest. Some of the older stags, that live out their entire lives on the open mountain, move into remote cliffs, as for example Ullauns, where, occupying sheltered ledges, with backs to a rock face and chewing the cud, they can survey the countryside below them and discern danger from afar. The occasional stag can be found asleep on such cliff ledges, curled up amongst the furze. Red deer are adept at finding shelter and at selecting a location that is dry and snug. Such lairs are surprisingly calm at ground level, even though there is a breeze only a metre or so above. On the open mountain deer seek out boulders and hollows, or may bed down on a little bench, facing the evening sunshine.

The red deer seem to be able to detect a coming thaw, and move out and uphill from sheltered woodland edges even before the snows have melted or the ground has become soft. Sometimes the animals can be seen in January up to about 500 metres, with the ground still frozen, but with a thaw on the way. When the thaw comes, it comes swiftly in Killarney, and sudden mildness and rain will quickly melt the snow. Red deer that I have observed during a thaw seemed to be startled by the swish of snow sliding off holly-tree branches and falling on to the woodland floor with a soft whoosh; it is not a sound to which they were accustomed. Vegetation newly freed of snow is relished. Now the deer, whose winter coats stood out against the background of white, merge into the yellows, fawns and light browns of the mountain, so that it is all too easy to assume that "all the deer" have left the hills and have crowded into the woodlands and lowlands. Especially in heavy snowfalls, such as occurred on 28 January 1984, deer may pack into the scattered areas of mixed woods, but that is primarily for shelter. They do not remain there for long, simply because there is no ground vegetation available for them in the few patches of woodland which remain on the lower slopes.

A January thaw may be no more than temporary; and while the feral goats which occupy the steep cliffs of some of these mountains are already dropping kids, and then mating, the mountain red deer are by no means rid of winter, but face an even harsher period ahead.

V

Deep Winter

Fuitt co bráth!
Is mó in doinenn ar cách;
is ob cách etriche an,
ocus is loch lán cach áth.

Forever cold!
Foul weather is even worse;
each bright stream is a river,
each ford is a lake.

Irish poem, 10th century[1]

By early February more people are out and about and, as daylight has noticeably lengthened, there are excellent opportunities of seeing red deer in the pastures and lowlands of Killarney. It is the time when wild garlic, with its haunting aroma, first sprouts beneath the beech trees on Ross Island. This island, accessed by a bridge and close to the town itself, generally holds some six or so deer in winter. They are more visible now, when the bracken is dead and the trees are still bare. These lowland reds are a darker colour than the mountain animals, whose winter coats are bleached by light and the elements. However, their darker coats sometimes make the lowland deer difficult to see against the swampy grounds of the wet alder woods.

This is also a good time to see the lowland red deer leaping. It is neither the length nor the height of the leap that impresses so much as the effortless way in which it is executed, for red deer jump with consummate ease. A hind, who has been quietly grazing near a fence, first rears up on her back legs, folding her front legs tightly against her body, and then pushes off, gracefully arching up and over the fence. As her head and forequarters clear the top, she unfolds her forelegs to take the impact of landing, at the same time pulling her back legs up tightly against her body to clear the fence. As her hind legs reach the ground, she is already grazing again, as if nothing whatsoever had happened. A running stag is every bit as graceful, clearing a 2-metre fence effortlessly, landing with precision and continuing his stride without interruption. A stag leaps with the same fluidity of motion as a dolphin curves out of the sea.

But for all the attractions of lush grasslands, brambles and browse of young trees, the lowlands also take their toll. Deer are killed on the roads, and many of those which trespass on farmland or the golf course are live-captured – only Park and Wildlife staff may do this legally – and removed. Trespass and depredations on private lands are an inevitable consequence of the increase in numbers in recent years. It is worth pointing out, however, that the National Park, which adjoins these private lands, is the only lowland sanctuary now left to the red deer, and as such is crucial not only to the lowland herd itself but also to the seasonal migrations to and from the mountains.

Some of the lowland habitats are exceptional. The red deer near Killarney Golf Course at times occupy a narrow strip of reed beds, no more than 50–100 metres wide, along the northern shore of Lough Leane, where they splash about in the shallow water between the islands, some scarcely big enough to lie upon. The deer also live in the wet alder woods between the reed beds and the adjoining pasture land and golf course. A few individuals can be found on the larger islands in Lough Leane, such as Innisfallen and Brown Islands, with Innisfallen being possibly the only island, apart from Ross, to hold a few deer throughout the winter.

In the mountains it is a different world, and only in exceptional years is February relatively mild. As family units make long treks each day in search of the precious greens, the family group as always led by the dominant hind. In such units, young stags bring up the rear, driving on the yearlings and calves with threatening gestures of their antlers, or kicks. A mother will still groom her calf, using her tongue to lick its face, ears, throat and breast. For a late-born calf this is a very telling time. One such calf which I watched on 1 February 1986, on the slopes of Cloughfune, was tiny, weak and lacked the vigour of a healthy calf. Its mother was exceptionally old looking, moved slowly and stiffly, as if her joints were arthritic, and her whole appearance was ragged, and her muzzle grizzled with age. Even if such a calf, whether male or female, were to survive its critical first winter, its eventual chances of becoming dominant, and therefore breeding successfully, would be low[2].

What really tell now are days of cold, continuous rain. The intensity of rain and hail storms in February is a special experience for the deer watcher, and one not easily forgotten. Rainfall is now heaviest and most prolonged, and its effects are aggravated by the deer being already two months into the winter. And there is the incessant wind, continuing to drain away energy and burning brown the exposed vegetation.

The winter of 1985–86 was long and hard, and that February one of the coldest on record. The mountains were clouded, swept by a bitterly cold east wind and mottled with snow. Loughs were frozen, and the vegetation withered brown. Nevertheless, there were red deer on the mountains, and I recorded them up to about 500 metres on frozen ground among snow patches throughout the month. In fact they appeared to cope surprisingly well with such severe conditions, and some of the main standbys were the extensive stands of furze on the lower south and south-west facing slopes. Hinds, calves and stags all crowded in together, neatly cropping the thorny tips. One old stag who frequented the furze stands of Cloughfune availed of both food and shelter together, nibbling the bushes about him while he was lying down, almost out of sight, deep amidst the furze.

Plate 53 A stag seeks winter greens amidst the snow-dusted furze of Cloughfune

Plate 54   Typical red deer family, led by dominant hind through winter snows

Plate 55   Red hinds ascend windswept ridges seeking exposed vegetation during snow lie

Plate 56   A sika doe's short legs slow her down in heavy snow on Cores Mountain

Plate 57   Sika does forage in a snow blizzard; Cromagloun Mountain

Plate 58   A hind reaches to browse holly; c. 200 metres, Crinneagh area

Plate 59   An example of bark stripping by deer within Tower Woods, Cloughfune area

Plate 60   Poachers in action: a young sika doe is being carried off the mountain, Ullauns area

Plate 61   One of the large secretive lowland stags amongst the wet alder woods

Plate 62   Red deer hind amidst the reed beds at Lough Leane's water edge - the most difficult area to stalk and photograph wild deer

Plate 63   Red deer calf cropping furze, Torc Mountain

Plate 64   Sensing a thaw, stags go uphill on Torc's snow-covered southern slopes

Plate 65   Red stags and sika, showing size and colour difference; Cloughfune area

Plate 66   In winter, the pelage of sika assumes a rich glossy black

Plate 67   Hearing is the more important sense when feeding amidst tall vegetation. A red hind on Torc's north slopes

Plate 68   An old stag, with antlers typically "gone back" during the October rut

Plate 69   Skull and antlers of the same stag that perished during the succeeding hard winter

Plate 70 *Hind and yearling on the south slopes of Torc, as the first greens of spring emerge*

Plate 71 *A tagged stag, antlers cast, amidst rhododendron infested alder woods; Reen area*

Plate 72   Park Ranger Peter O'Toole tagging newly-born red deer calf in the Cores Mountain area

Plate 73   A strong calf, just tagged, still nibbles grass, though sedated, in the lowland pastures

Plate 74   Dr Jim Larner examines a stag he has just tagged in the lowland pastures

Plate 75   Examining the remains of a stag with antlers entangled in an old deer fence, on the cliffs of Failacurrane

Plate 76   His antlers entangled in the vines of clematis, the carcass of a stag amidst the woods of Muckross

Plate 77   Natural mortality: a hind's carcass amidst molinia *tussocks; Crinneagh area*

Plate 78   The hind that hanged herself, reaching for holly; Stompacoumeen area

Plate 79   A lingering death: the snagged hind leg of a red deer calf in sheep wire; Mangerton Slieve area

Plate 80   Hind drowned in waterfall; Crinneagh area

The diversity of the mountain habitat is important for winter survival. Innumerable small and shallow hollows, rock escarpments, large boulders and cuttings by mountain streams all provide vital shelter. Equally essential now to survival is the reserve of body fat built up in the previous summer. Towards the end of the month, some deer are probably already in negative energy balance[3] – they are using up more energy in trekking to gather food than the available food itself can provide. Hinds will fight for food, standing on their back legs, facing each other and boxing with their forefeet, just as stags do when they have cast their antlers. One of the possible reasons for the sika's success, and rapid spread throughout Killarney, may be its ability, in these conditions to utilise and convert into energy the withered, straw-like fionaun, their digestive system being especially efficient in this[4].

Death may strike at any time, but from now on evidence of natural mortality is more frequent than in any other season. Carcasses on the mountain quickly disappear. Fox, raven and grey crow, all expert scavengers, leave nothing to waste. But mortality has not yet peaked; there are still many weeks of severe weather ahead.

By March, there is spectacular contrast between the lowlands and the mountain habitat. The mildness of the Killarney lowlands is already evident early in the month; grass growth has commenced with rising temperatures, and garden lawns have received their first cut of the year. The earliest warblers arrive before the month's end for spring nesting, and commercial life bustles with the prospect of another tourist season. There are also changes in the mountains: lengthening daylight and rising temperatures result in a gradual increase in activity and appetite for the red deer. But it is still winter, with temperatures sufficiently low to prevent new growth. As yet there are no fresh greens, and they will not appear in quantity for a further two months.

Feeding on withered vegetation, together with longer treks to obtain greens, and the intense grazing competition between red deer, sika and sheep, can be telling. In the afternoon and evening grazings, the concentration of red deer in the furze of Cloughfune, south-west Torc, and also on the mountain stream inches of Inchabuailenmbo (Mangerton – Stompacoumeen) is noticeably greater than in summer. The mountain red deer manage to cope. They are truly wild, with many centuries of adaptation to the their environment. They are also free-ranging, and that is vitally important; freedom to travel gives opportunity of habitat choice. Their density is also lower in winter.

March is the month when the fully mature and older stags shed their antlers. An antler is cast by breaking off naturally from the pedicle, the point of fracture always being below the *burr*, or *coronet*, the ring of bone at the base of the antler where it joins the pedicle. Antlers are generally cast one at a time, and for a few days a stag goes about with a single antler. Younger stags carry their antlers until April or May. On very rare occasions a stag may keep his antlers, white and bleached from the winter's rains, into July or August; this is an abnormality. The earliest antler casting I observed in the mountain herd was by a mature stag on 22 February 1986; which incidentally was a severe winter and a particularly cold February. Sika bucks shed their antlers in the same way and at about the same time as red deer.

Each antler casting carries with it a small portion of the pedicle beneath, so that an old stag's pedicles may be reduced in length, but not in circumference, which increases with age. One tradition has it that a young stag's cast antlers have a convex, or slightly bulbous shape at the point of fracture below the burr; that in a stag in his prime, this point of fracture is about level; and that in an old stag it becomes concave. It is not known if this invariably holds true, but almost all of the cast antlers of younger stags which I have found had slightly bulbous fracture points, while those of older stags are generally level.

Immediately after casting, the new antlers begin to grow at the pedicle tops. Growth extends across the entire pedicle, so that the antler is at its full width from the start. The initial growth is known as the "gooseberry" stage, for that is what it looks like – soft, bulbous and covered in velvet. If an antler is found very shortly after shedding, traces of fresh blood will be seen on the point of fracture. One authority suggests that this "wound", and wound healing, is necessary to initiate growth of the new antler[5]. If it is not found quickly, then the chances of securing it intact in the Killarney mountains are slight, for antlers are quickly chewed by both stags and hinds. An indication of the craving for minerals by deer in the mountains is that whole skeletons, apart from the larger pieces of vertebrae, quickly disappear. Of a large stag's antlers only the hard nobs surrounding the coronet itself may remain. Red deer will also chew material other than bone. On occasions I have found, on the slopes of Mangerton, the aluminium struts of weather balloons gnawed by deer. In sharp contrast, antlers dropped in the lowlands, which are limestone based, are generally found intact, or with few signs of chewing. Some antlers lie untouched in the Killarney lowland woods for at least a year. Interestingly, the cast antlers I found on the island of Inishvicillaun, off the coast of Kerry, were likewise unchewed; this is described more fully in Appendix 3.

Cast antlers are much sought after by walkers on the hills and lowlands. Generally, there is no difficulty in distinguishing those of sika from red deer, which are bigger, heavier and have more points. However, there is some similarity between a *young* red stag's and those of a mature sika buck, though the configuration of the top tines differs significantly, and with experience it becomes easy enough to tell which is which. One convenient and simple method I have found is to compare the angle between the brow tine and beam; almost always the angle in a sika's antler is noticeably narrower (more acute) than in a stag's. In my collection of antlers, found both in the mountains and lowlands of Killarney, the average angle for red stags was 104 degrees; the average for sika bucks was 68 degrees.

By March most of the snows, except on the high tops, have melted, leaving the vegetation clean-washed and surprisingly brightly coloured, a joy to behold. The mountain streams foam white with melt water. Red deer will go high in March; in mid-March I have recorded stag groups at about 650 metres on Mangerton. On 26 March 1989 there were four sika at 600 metres on Mangerton when hard-packed snow patches still covered the slopes, and a concentration of 20 red deer plus a further six sika at 450 metres. Towards the end of the month, many red stags, hinds and yearlings are found on the summits and ridge-tops from Torc to Poulagower. Sometimes only hinds and followers are seen, with no stags visible.

Mountain weather can still be, and often is, severe; March is the month of east winds, sweeping in from the Continent, bringing a numbing cold that cuts body heat and saps energy and can persist for many days, sometimes weeks. Fat reserves are now vital, as is good health and the mobility to search for food. Inevitably there are mortalities, and mortality will shortly peak.

VI

Spring

Ní chotail in eilit máel
ac búirfedaig fó brecláeg;
  do-gní rith tar barraib tor;
    ní déin 'na hadbaid cotal.

The hornless hind does not sleep, crying for her speckled fawn; she
runs over the top of bushes; she sleeps not in her lair.

Irish poem, c. 1150 A.D.[1]

By April the deer are obviously more active, although some may now be on their
last reserves of fat. But as yet there is no significant new growth of greens on the
hills and, after a particularly severe winter, the heather is browned and dry from
wind-burn. Grazing competition between red deer, sika and sheep is more intense.
Often the inches and flushes are by now cropped down to bare earth. It is the time
when deer trespass most on farmland and the inevitable conflict means that some of
these animals will never again see Killarney. They are captured and moved out to other
parks, or sold off to commercial deer farms as breeding stock. It is certain that some
are poached, but the numbers are unknown.

Some days in April can be very mild, and warm weather envelopes the mountains,
with prolonged sunshine and little wind. Such conditions result in haze, when the hills
shimmer and become blue outlines. In mountain loughs, waterlilies begin to grow
afresh and can be seen beneath the surface, curling upwards from the peaty depths. It
is suddenly like spring on the hill, and the red deer, still in full winter coat, lie up on
south facing slopes after feeding, panting in the heat, with mouths open and tongues
lolling to cool themselves. A warm, dry spell like this may last for several days, sometimes
a week or more, bringing with it extremely dangerous conditions. In the hills which
border the National Park with its red deer habitat, sheepmen regularly burn off old
heather about now so as to encourage new growth, or fires may be lit by picnickers.
Winds can suddenly rise, spreading the fires, and after a warm spell, the withered
mountain vegetation is as dry as tinder. A mountain fire now in the National Park has
the potential for catastrophe.

Since 1980, there have been at least four major (and many minor) mountain fires in Killarney National Park, which burned out heather, dwarf furze and withered grasses. By far the most serious was the great fire of 1984, from 25–27 April, when an estimated 1,600 hectares of mountain habitat were consumed. There were two fire centres. One was on Mangerton, on the slopes above and south of Failacurrane; this was extinguished in a day. The other started on the north shores of the Long Range and quickly spread, incinerating the vegetation on the Eagle's Nest Mountain, also that on slopes to the north, and then up and over the summit of Shehy Mountain, which probably held the most important heather stands of the park. It swept onwards, burning much of Coumcloughane north of Shehy, until finally, through lack of fuel, it was extinguished on the high scree slopes of Toamies. Had it gone southwards, crossing the Killarney-Kenmare roadway, and spread into the main red deer range on Torc-Mangerton, the effects on the red deer and their habitat would have been catastrophic. It is likely that this fire was started accidentally by tourists. All mountain fires have a potential danger for wildlife, and though red deer are swift and could outrun a fire, once driven out from the sanctuary of the park, deer would be more prone to exploitation and many would never return.

Fire itself is a natural phenomenon, and the burning off of old vegetation, leaving ash deposits, encourages fresh grass growth. In the early 1970s, some carefully controlled, experimental burns were tried on the mountains of the park, to study the effects on the vegetation and the red deer[2]. Prior to this, in the 1960s, and probably also in the early 1950s, some fires had been deliberately started outside the park so as to stimulate fresh growth in order to entice deer away from their haven. Fire management is a complex subject: knowing when and what to burn. And in the mountains, because of wind, there is always the problem of controlling a fire, especially at Killarney, which takes the brunt of the Atlantic westerlies.

Unlike grass, furze does not seem to recover quickly on the hillsides. Following a mountain fire in the Cloughfune area, the furze took several years to regenerate, and sika that usually occupied this area appeared there less frequently thereafter, perhaps due in part to the lack of cover, though there was also sustained culling of sika at that time.

In April, the lowland woods begin to green. Soon the bluebells will flower, and the first sika calves appear, a measure of the contrast between lowlands and mountains. Such early calves are dropped in the sheltered field systems of the Muckross Peninsula.

As appetites increase, stags and hinds will turn to anything palatable. As well as antlers and bones, red deer take carrion and have been recorded pulling dead rabbits from snares and eating them[3]. A hind which I observed in the mountains in the third week of April 1982 approached a frog that had jumped near her and, with raised foreleg, deliberately tried to strike it down. However, it is uncanny how, even in conditions as lean as this, the deer can differentiate between edible and poisonous plants. One of the first shoots to appear on the lower mountain slopes is the Irish spurge. Its bright green leaves and light yellow flower heads stand out against the whitened mountain grasses and look attractive, but it is poisonous, and although starved of greens, the deer will not touch it. Similarly, the leaves of foxgloves, also toxic, are left uneaten, though any grasses about them in the old field systems on the lower slopes are grazed to the earth, and right up to the foxgloves.

In the mountains, in an exceptionally mild winter, the earliest greens may begin to appear by about mid-April, but in many years there may still be none until a month later. The severe weather is by no means over. A good illustration of this is that on the summits and ridges of the higher mountains, outside the National Park, snow cover may linger on to the end of May. It can happen that the few days of balmy weather in April are no more than a false spring. Even towards the end of the month it can still be harsh, with a sudden drop in temperature, prolonged cold, driving rain and, on the higher slopes, hail. In these conditions, the hail coalesces and freezes at about 600 metres, creating a mosaic of white and brown. It is an indication of how well adapted the deer are, when they are able to wrest a living from the mountain slopes in such conditions.

Such a cold, blustery period at this time is called the "Scariveen", from *Scairbhín na gCuach* (the blustery period of the cuckoos). Like many of the phrases in the Irish language describing nature, it is both pertinent and accurate; it is about now that the cuckoos are first heard in the countryside. This weather pattern is simply an inconvenience in the city, but in the mountains, it can be particularly cold and telling. For the hill deer, some of whom are now on their last reserves, it is life or death. Mortality is likely to peak now, and while few carcasses may be found, most are located at this time. Deer usually expire on the lower slopes, in valley bottoms near streamsides and amongst furze, rushes and tall heather, where presumably the animals had sought shelter.

Wild deer die for various reasons. The young, especially calves, are particularly vulnerable, and a Scottish study showed that about a third of the summer calf drop dies off in its first year, mortality being higher in males than in females[4]. Old and sick animals are also obviously vulnerable. Tooth wear in old animals is ultimately fatal, as a deer that cannot graze and masticate its food is under a death sentence. Deer succumb from parasites such as liver fluke, from pneumonia and perhaps a few from pellet wounds inflicted by poachers.

It is possible that the final moments of natural death come on the open hillside from hypothermia. Hypothermia, often called the "silent killer", is a condition well known to mountain walkers and climbers, caused by low ambient temperature and exhaustion. Essentially it is a drop the body's core temperature, resulting in a stupor of insensibility. Observers who have seen red deer actually go down in the mountains have commented on the surprising speed with which it finally happens, which points to hypothermia.

Sometimes it is possible to identify old or diseased red deer in the mountains as being marked for death. An old stag which I photographed during the October rut in 1979 had distinctive antlers which had gone back, so that his few points had an unmistakable shape. The animal then looked alert and strong, but the following winter was hard, with over half a metre of snow on Mangerton on 23 February. It was his last; his skeleton was found the following spring by Wildlife Warden Paudie O'Leary, and we confirmed his identity from photographs. Similarly, a photograph of a hind on 26 February 1989, preceded by two days of deep snow on the hill, revealed a telltale swelling of the throat, which may have been the result of liver fluke. Such an animal would probably have succumbed late in that spring, though she could have survived a further year.

This is a natural cull, the removal by the environment of those members of the herd least fitted to survive the rigours of a mountain winter. It is quite a different cull to that artificially imposed during the nineteenth and early twentieth centuries on the red deer of Killarney for sporting and commercial purposes, when stags were stalked by the wealthier classes and shot in their prime so as to acquire *trophy heads* – those with the largest and most elaborate antlers.

Before April is out, some of the migrant birds have already returned to the hills. Wheatears come to the lower slopes and will breed in the same boulder fields as the resident stonechats. Sandpipers fly in to the pebble shorelines of mountain loughs. The wild geese have long since departed. May, which will bring the first evidence of the mountain spring, is at hand.

Generally, it is mid-May before greens are available on the hills. For some, the weakest and least fit, it is too late, and they succumb as the first shoots appear. This is particularly so after a long hard winter. A yearling hind was found by wildlife wardens in May 1986 on the lakeshore by Toamies Wood, barely skin and bone. She died in their hands. Carcasses are still found in May and sometimes a few into early June.

Calves that have made it through the winter are now yearlings, and, if strong and fit are well on their way to normal survival and fecundity. The benefit of prolonged lactation is obvious now. The latest dates that I have seen yearlings suckle in the mountains were from the 23 May to 12 June. A yearling male that is exceptionally strong has now grown almost as large as his mother.

As new green growth pushes up the mountain slopes, more and more deer concentrate on it. Families begin to coalesce, and group size grows from the normal three, four or five, to as many as 30 to 40. So great is the urge to feed now, that something unknown in other seasons may is seen on the hill: all heads are down together, avidly grazing. This confirms that a grazing deer's first line of defence is its hearing, since its nose is buried in the thick grass, which may reach well above its eyes. Scent does not travel through vegetation at ground level, but is carried up higher, in the wind. Once disturbance is detected, the deer are instantly alert, heads up and long necks stretched high, so as to concentrate all three senses of hearing, sight and smell on the source of danger, to identify both its location and what it is. Later in the summer deer graze among tussocks of purple moor-grass which can reach as high as their backs.

As May draws to an end, the red deer appear unkempt and ragged. The heavy winter coat is coming off in bunches, to be replaced later by the sleeker and redder summer pelage. Spring is in the air, and soon it will be June, and the season for calving. But, before May is finally out, one or two red calves may already have been dropped on the hills.

With the coming of June, the stags are also feeding voraciously. In addition to the demands of growing antlers, the deficit of previous months must be made good. Scottish research in the 1970s[5] revealed that a mature stag that rutted successfully, perhaps loosing 15–20% of his body weight in the process, might shed a further 15% if the following winter was particularly hard.

Calving peaks early in June. The yeld hinds are now very strong and soon will be in full summer coat. Hinds that calve may look ragged and are still in winter pelage, the foetus having first call on the mother's reserves. Such hinds are sometimes misjudged to be in poor condition, although their appearance may be the result of a greater investment of energy in the young, and it may well be, therefore, that they are the better mothers. By now, the sika in the mountains have also had calves, as they generally commence to drop in May, earlier than the red deer.

By early June, the fresh green growth has pushed up to the summits. Pregnant hinds, preparing for parturition, have begun to break away from family groups, and with the birth of new calves, the yearly cycle, and also the life cycle, of these wild red deer are completed, and begin all over again.

Appendices

I
Calf Tagging

Tagging red deer in the lowlands has been accomplished more successfully than on the hill, due to easier access by four-wheel-drive vehicles in favourable weather. It is carried out by night with the aid of powerful spotlights. The placing of the immobilising dart in the animal, and the subsequent reviving dart, is only done by specially authorised park staff. Some reactions of the darted red deer are noteworthy. On 18 February 1994, when I witnessed six calves and one hind being darted, a similar reaction was displayed by each of the seven deer. After the initial jump when the dart struck, they recommenced grazing, and when the immobilising chemical took effect and they fell down, they continued to nibble the grass from a prone position. Gathering of grass by nibbling continued while their ears were being tagged, and also throughout while the antidote was being administered. This reaction was evident in all of the six calves, but not to the same extent in the hind. In one case, the darted calf was repeatedly mounted by another calf on four to five occasions before the darted calf went down.

Tagging has resulted in accurate information on deer movements within the lowland habitats, as well as the extent of home ranges for individual deer. It has also provided factual information on the movements to and from the uplands during summer and the October rut. The pattern which has emerged is movement to and from the Muckross area, whereas the Knockreer area is holding an essentially discrete population.

Tagging in the upland herd has of necessity been confined to calves. The survival rate and movement of calves, and the longevity of individual mountain-bred red deer will for the first time become available as tagging progresses. One hind, tagged as a calf on the hill in 1984, still survived eleven years later and had a new-born calf running with her in June 1995. In time, mortality finds of known-age animals will also provide an accurate standard against which visual assessment and analysis of tooth wear as an estimation of age can be compared.

The provision of accurate information, as distinct from speculation and bias, is essential for management of the Killarney red deer and takes precedence over the understandable disappointment sometimes expressed by hill walkers on seeing tagged wild deer on the hills and by tourists seeing them in the lowland woods and pastures.

II
Mortality

Prior to the systematic searching for and recording of winter mortality in the mountains of Killarney National Park, begun by Park Ranger Peter O'Toole in the winter of 1993–94, natural mortality figures of the red deer had not been established. The number of mortalities recorded in previous winters amounted to about five carcasses in some years only. Searching for carcasses demands day-long mountain walking over the winter period. Wild deer natural deaths are nothing like the spectacular deaths of sheep on the mountains, as exemplified during the late winter and early spring of 1986[1]. When found, in some cases weather was already covering the carcass in hailstones or snow, so that a short time later it would have been invisible from about 2 metres away. Any red deer carcass found could safely be described as of recent occurrence; known mortality remains are so quickly disposed of by the population of foxes, ravens and grey crows that only the larger leg bones, with some vertebrae, remain after approximately three to four weeks. An example of the speed with which the remains of a hind's carcass was scavenged has already been described in Chapter One. Many similar examples exist. Even with daily searching, a carcass may not be located until several days after death, by which time it is too late to determine the animal's sex in the case of dead calves, but in the case of stags, antlers when present are a sure diagnostic feature. Young males in the mountains rarely have grown pedicles by yearling stage.

Causes of death were found to be in part due to accidents. Examples are many. The hind who hanged herself had evidently taken a step too far along the projecting limb of a holly tree growing out from the cliff face, then slipped and fell, catching her jaws in a fork of the tree. It is possible that the hind which was jammed between rocks and a tree stump in a waterfall, again illustrated, was also a victim of stretching too far for a holly bush growing at the top of the falls. At least these accidents resulted in quick deaths. Not so the stag whose forefoot was caught in the holly tree fork. He had obviously reached up on his back legs to browse the leaves, while steadying himself with a forefoot against the tree, when his foot slipped into the tree fork. The more he pulled to extricate his foot, the tighter his foot had jammed. A similar situation occurred to one of the feral goats, which also resulted in death. The death of a young male calf, tagged in the mountains during the previous summer and thus a known age of eight months and two weeks, was caused by not fully clearing the top straining wire as he jumped one of the many sheep fences which cross the lower hillsides, and as his trailing hind foot was caught between the top and second top wire, the twisting action effectively created a wire snare from which he hung by the leg, and died a slow death. Similarly, a red deer calf whose hind leg was caught in the wire mesh of old sheep fencing in the lowlands was luckily found by chance and released in July 1991; the parent hind had waited near by. There are other, more rare, instances of mortalities due also to man-made hazards, as for example when a red deer in the lowlands was drowned in an artificial pool in Killarney Golf Course[2].

The majority of natural mortalities in the mountains cannot be ascribed with certainty to a specific cause, but probably result from hypothermia and pneumonia in the mountain winter, especially in winters with prolonged, heavy rainfall. There is evidence that some predation occurs to an animal that is dying. A yearling stag, just growing pedicles, which Peter O'Toole and I found dead high on the slopes of Coumeen, had his head twisted sideways on the ground, and his exposed eye was already picked out by a raven or grey crow. He was still in *rigor mortis*, and thus had died in this position. When examined, the unexposed eye underneath, and pressed to the ground, was also found to have been picked out, indicating that this must have occurred before the animal was fully dead. When the eyes are gone, a deer is certain to die; it is one way by which scavengers can ensure that carrion will be available. This finding was no surprise, as sometimes ravens and grey crows can be observed following an injured animal about. During one October rut, while observing a hind on the hill who had an injured leg and was badly limping, it was noticeable that as she moved about the hillside, followed by a stag, she was also followed from place to place by a pair of grey crows that perched about 50 metres away, just waiting. However, that hind survived, and successfully reared a calf the following summer. Actual predation of calves by foxes has been reported, one instance being an attack by a fox on a sika calf witnessed in Killarney National Park[3]. Remains of very small calves, probably sika, have been found close to fox earths while searching for and tagging calves of red deer; these, of course, may have been carrion that was scavenged from natural deaths.

The results of the two year's winter mortality survey are given below.

Table 1. Winter Mortality in the Mountain Herd of Red Deer in Killarney National Park

	Totals	Stags	Hinds	Calves	?
1993–94	39	9	19	6	5
1994–95	40	4	18	17	1

Obviously recorded mortality was a minimum figure only, as all dead animals were not located, due to the rapidity with which remains disappear and the extent and ruggedness of the terrain. After about mid-May, when the new growth of *molinia* has commenced and is greening the hills, the only carcass likely to be found would be a late mortality. Natural deaths, therefore, must be assumed to account for more losses than those actually recorded.

Red deer mortality in the lowlands is remarkable in that so few carcasses have been found. In 1994, three red deer and six sika deer were reported killed by vehicle impact on the roads. Lowland stags are prone to death from the entanglement of their antlers in strands of *clematis*, a garden escape which festoons some of the woodland trees. In recent years, six stags have been found dead with antlers thus entangled; one was found alive and freed by park staff. These lowland deaths are not included in the mountain mortality figures.

Research on disease in the Killarney red deer has been based on results from those animals shot or removed because of injury resulting from road accidents, or were causing damage to private property. So far, the results have proved negative in respect of diseases harmful or threatening to man or livestock. Research into the parasites of the Killarney red deer, and into the red deer in Glenveigh National Park in County Donegal, has revealed healthy populations[4]. The presence of nasal bot-fly in the Donegal red deer[5] is considered to be a consequence of that herd being derived from introductions from Scotland, where nasal bot-fly is common; nasal bot-fly has not been recorded in the native Killarney red deer. Lyme disease, associated with wild deer but not exclusive to them as hosts of the vectors[6], was found in 1989 to be absent from 60 Irish deer tested[7], and has not been recorded in the Killarney red deer. Tuberculosis has been recorded in Wicklow deer[8]; about 3% infection was recorded in the wild sika in Wicklow, and about 4% in the fallow deer of Phoenix Park, Dublin[9]. Tuberculosis was reported in only one case out of over 1,000 sika culled in Killarney in a ten year period; it has not been recorded in the Killarney red deer.

III
The Red Deer of Killarney
on Inishvicillaun

Red deer of the native Killarney stock were established on Inishvicillaun, one of the Blasket Islands off the Kerry coast. The island is the property of Mr Charles J. Haughey, former Taoiseach. These deer originated from four animals, a stag and three hinds, transferred there from Killarney in 1980. Between then and 1991 there have been transfers of a further seven red deer, three stags and four hinds, from Killarney to the island. As far as is known, natural mortality had accounted for at least seven deer up to 1991: three stags, three hinds and one calf. There may well have been other unrecorded mortalities.

There is no known precedent of wild Killarney red deer being left to fend for themselves on a small island, approximately 200 acres or 0.8 square kilometres in extent, about eight sea miles from the mainland, and at the extreme western edge of Europe; only An Tiaracht, the furthest offshore of the Blaskets, is further west.

The Inishvicillaun herd presented an important opportunity of assessing its performance in a unique situation. I visited the island on three brief occasions; the visits lasting one day on 3 April 1990, and three days each on 13–15 November 1990, and 23–25 July 1991. The counts of red deer on the island are summarised below.

Table 2. Red Deer numbers on Inishvicillaun

	Totals	Stags	Hinds	Calves
1990				
3 April	25	4	16	5
13–15 November	32	8	17	7
1991				
23–25 July	40	13	19	8

The addition of seven calves (of 1990) by November, which, when added to the April count of 25, corresponded with the November count of 32, implied that no mortality had occurred, though in fact one hind had died in the meantime (discussed below). This meant that one deer at least was overlooked in that April count; a good illustration of the wildness of the island. The count of 40 on the following July, increased by the eight calves (of the same year – 1991), implied that all seven calves of the previous year had survived. This would be exceptional in the Killarney mountain herd.

Fecundity could be accurately assessed for the November 1990 and the July 1991 counts, as the recruitment of yearlings to hind numbers (from the previous years' calves) meant that there were 16 and 17 hinds of breeding age with which to compare their calf drops of seven and eight, respectively. This resulted in a calf to hind ratio of 0.44 and 0.47; lower than those recorded in the Killarney lowland herd, but almost twice as high as the Killarney mountain herd. This says much for the island's pastures and climate. A special feature of the counts was the high number of males to females in the calves born, which was evident from the recruitment shown in the following counts. The five calves recorded in April 1990 (almost yearlings by then) had, by the November 1990 count, increased the number of stags by four, and the number of hinds by one; the seven calves dropped in 1990 turned out to be five males and two females, having increased the number of stags by five, and the number of hinds by two, in the July 1991 count. Scottish research on red deer in Rhum has shown that large hinds have more male than female calves. While one year's count is far too insufficient to generalise for Inishvicillaun, certainly some of the hinds observed there were large animals.

The island is an elevated plateau surrounded by cliffs up to 120 metres in height. Its climate is hyperoceanic; in strong winds, which were frequent, salt spray went right over the island's summits. The weather can be severe; during the 3 April 1990 visit, hail showers were frequent, with one fall of snow. However, the influence of the Atlantic is all-pervading, and the hail and snow quickly melted. The exposure to wind was severe on exposed level tops and windward slopes. The red deer had become well accustomed to finding shelter in the lee of many rock outcrops, in nooks and sheltered hollows low down on lee slopes and in among the cliffs. Overall, the island enjoys a long growth period. In mid-November 1990 lush green grass still grew on 70–80% of the island. It is possible that its vegetation also has a high nutrient value. There are references in the Blasket literature to the richness of the island's grazing and soil, which may result from salt spray, and weathering of volcanic rock outcrops. In spring and summer a colony of great black-backed gulls occupies sloping ground on the western side of the island, and gull colonies have been shown to have had a beneficial effect on the performance of red deer in Scotland[1].

The richness of the island's grazing, when compared to the mountain habitat of the parent Killarney red deer herd, was neatly illustrated by the finding of five cast antlers, three in April and two in November 1990, all of which lay exposed on the open ground and were in part covered by growing vegetation, with incipient lichen on some antlers. These were at least a year on the ground, and were intact, unchewed, something which would be unheard of in the Killarney hills, where cast antlers and skeleton bones are chewed down to stumps. Other cast antlers previously found and preserved in the dwelling house on the island also showed no signs of chewing. The size and weight of one island antler was intermediate between those of a Killarney mountain and a Killarney lowland red deer, as set out below:

Killarney mountain cast antler	880 grams
Inishvicillaun cast antler	1620 grams
Killarney lowland cast antler	2340 grams

Winter is the crucial time for wild red deer, and on the 3 April 1990 visit the impact of limited space and food was evident. The greens on south-facing slopes were grazed to the earth, much as the hillside flushes and streamside inches are at this time in the Killarney mountains. The deer on the island were observed cropping lichen, *Ramolina* species, on rock outcrops and on old stone fences; there was a distinct browse line on the lichen at deer grazing height on the large rocks and well-marked deer paths at their bases. Although not actually observed, it is also possible that the island deer may have chewed some of the carcasses of rabbits, the result of *myxomatosis* introduced to the island many years prior to its present occupancy; these rabbit carcasses were lying about and bore signs of chewing. It is not known if the island deer have had any impact on fledgling Manx shearwaters which, with storm petrels, nest in colonies on the island. Red deer in Scotland have been recorded as predators of Manx shearwaters[2].

There was, in April 1990, aggression among the older hinds, not uncommon among red deer in the fight for favoured food areas in wintertime. This aggression was not observed in November, when grass was plentiful and hinds were in peak condition. One natural mortality was found in November – an old hind that had probably died on the previous late April or May. She was aged at 19–20 years old by tooth analysis subsequently at UCD[3], and may well have been one of the original hinds transferred from Killarney in 1980. It must be one of, if not the oldest recorded Killarney red deer that has been accurately aged.

The red deer on Inishvicillaun had become accustomed to the noise and sight of a helicopter, scarcely giving it a second glance as one started up and took off, but typically were still wary of human presence, and were up and alert at the first sight of people, or the sound of human voices. Similarly, though they grazed close to the dwelling house in late evening and took little notice of people within, they were instantly alert if anyone moved outdoors – they are still wild deer.

Management of this herd in a unique situation has to be on a trial and error basis, monitored as the situation evolves year by year.

Plate 81   Greenland white-fronted geese, both seen and heard during the mountain winters

Plate 82 *A short-eared owl hiding (centre left) amidst sedges on Torc Mountain*

Plate 83 *Irish red deer on Inishvickillaun, descendants of those transferred from Killarney*

Plate 84   Golden plover, more frequently heard than seen during the October rut in the Killarney mountains

*Plate 85   A wren, frequently seen, and heard, up to the
summits of the highest of the Kerry mountains*

Plate 86   Evening sunshine warms a lizard on the stone fences of old field systems on Ferta Mountain

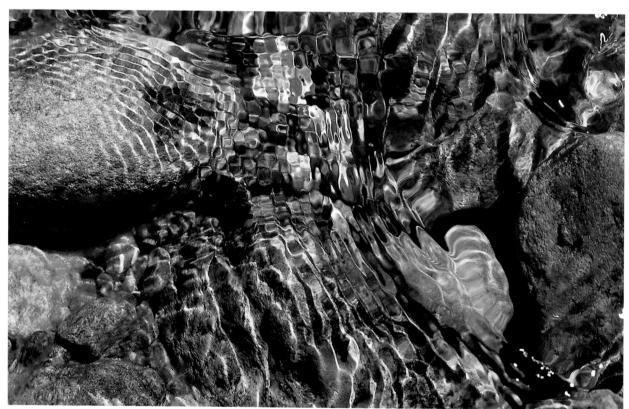

Plate 87   The crystal-clear waters of the Crinneagh Mountain stream

Plate 88   Fresh spring foliage at the edge of Muckross Lake

Plate 89   The Killarney Valley in summer, view from Torc Mountain

Plate 90   An aspen, flaming with autumn colours, is reflected on Killarney's Upper Lake

Plate 91   Killarney National Park in winter: looking west from Cores Mountain towards the Reeks

Plate 92   October storm clouds clearing over Cromagloun Mountain

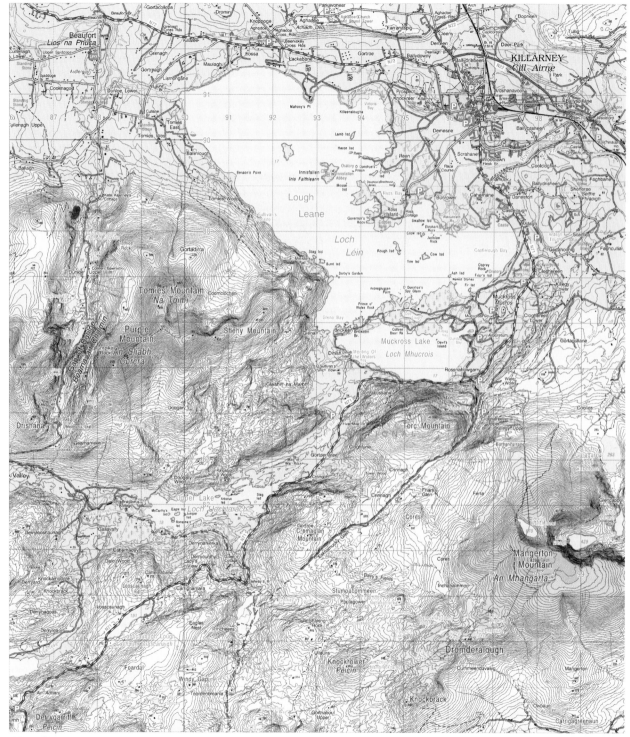

Plate 93   Map of the region

IV
Photographing the Wild Red Deer

The most important thing to remember in photographing wild red deer, or any wild animal, is that the wild animal comes first; the photograph is of secondary importance and should not be attempted at all if it involves serious disturbance. The second thing to remember is that it rains in Killarney; it rains a lot. Perhaps the single most useful gadget while photographing in the Killarney mountains is a plastic bag; two plastic bags, one inside the other, are even better, as strong winds will open the perforations and tears which are inevitable when crawling through heather and rough ground. What photographic equipment is best is a matter of personal preference, but reliability and portability are two essential requirements.

The importance of reliability is appreciated when eventually the moment comes of pressing the shutter release. In the Killarney mountains, this may only come after a long day on the hill and after up to eight or 10 hours of walking and careful stalking, by which time you are cold and wet, and the light is fast fading. One incident will illustrate this point. When I eventually photographed the stag "Growler", it had already taken three days of observation, watching his movements and judging how the varying wind directions contoured the mountain slopes. Finally, on the fourth day, at the end of a long wait throughout a cold and rainy October morning and afternoon, he came downhill, following his hinds, and presented a very brief opportunity, no more than about three seconds, in which to photograph him. After investing that amount of time and effort, it would have been devastating if the camera had not worked. It did, and I knew it would. When selecting equipment for wild deer photography, in my experience reliability is all important.

Portability means lightness. Lightweight equipment is appreciated at the day's end; it's not much use having a large and fast telephoto lens if its too heavy to carry all day in the mountains. Lightness effectively restricts film size to 35 mm format, and necessitates making a compromise between large aperture and light weight in telephoto lens choice. I have found a long focus lens (lighter than a telephoto lens), with a maximum aperture of f 6.8, to be quite adequate for most deer photography, even though its use is restricted in low light. Mountain walking, and crawling in a stalk, make a tripod more a hindrance than a help. A shoulder stock support is better, and there is generally a rock on which to steady the lens, or you can improvise with a backpack, or a rolled-up jacket. When calculating weight, remember that days on the hill will be long, and that food, fluid and survival gear, as well as adequate clothing, must also be carried.

Practically all wild deer photography in the mountains involves a stalk. Naturally it is necessary to stalk up-wind; deer have an excellent sense of smell. Deer also have an excellent sense of hearing. Stalking silently is usually recommended in photographic books and journals, as if it were possible. In practice, it is not. In my experience photographic stalking is more successful on windy days, when there are background noises of wind and wind-threshed vegetation. But whatever the conditions, stalking demands a code of behaviour which means that if it involves serious disturbance to the animal, don't do it.

In my opinion, there is only one type of stalking in wild deer photography that can be called successful, and that is to start sufficiently far away before the deer is aware of your presence, stalk into the deer, take the photograph, and then stalk back out again without the deer ever having been aware of your presence. This is easier said than done, because to at least half fill a frame it is usually necessary to stalk to within 35 to 40 metres of the animal. But practice helps. Several plates were photographed in this way. It takes a lot of time and experience to achieve it, and, in my experience, then only in about 30–40% of attempts. The best standards are those we set ourselves, because we will try and keep to them. Self-imposed discipline is the best discipline; it's the only discipline that costs nothing, and generally, it lasts.

After stalking into the deer, it is tempting for the beginner to try and grab a photograph before the animal alarms and runs off. Don't; wait, and let the deer settle, and take time to regain your normal breathing and composure. The deer will usually become instantly alert at the sound of the camera shutter; they can hear and distinguish a mechanical noise even in high winds. But if they do not locate the noise, and it is not repeated, they will usually settle again, and it should be possible to stalk away, undetected. Keeping as low down as possible is a good general rule, as a standing human figure is certain to alarm a wild deer. At dusk, when lying flat out on the ground, it has sometime occurred that a travelling deer will walk quite close by, unable to differentiate the human form from the rock outcrops and clumps of heather. This difficulty of separating the human from his surroundings can also occur when a deer, out in the open, is looking in at a woodland edge, trying to locate the unusual noise of a camera shutter.

Most opportunities of photographing wild deer are lost due to hurrying. Normally, I walk quickly to the general area where I know from experience the deer are likely to be, but when about two kilometres away, progression then becomes very slow. I would consider that from then on a kilometre an hour would be too fast. Binoculars are essential in locating the deer, and when located, if it is obvious that they are disturbed, then there is no point in stalking them. Try again another day. Stalking time varies, but, after the subject has been located, two to three hours would be a good average for a successful stalk. Some photographic magazines speak of luck in wildlife photography. In my experience, it is so rare that it scarcely matters. Wildlife photographers carry their luck around with them, on their backs and in their heads. It's knowledge, experience and lots of hard work and patience that get the results.

Having taken photographs of deer, it is just as important to be truthful. If the photograph was taken in an enclosed park, say so – you will be all the more respected for it. Photographs are regularly published of a red stag as representing wild deer, when it is patently obvious that the animal was photographed in an enclosed park, under controlled conditions. Contrived "wildlife" photographs sell well, and commercial pressures on professional photographers have resulted in these being a significant percentage of what is published. If my own collection of over 4,000 transparencies of the wild red deer of Killarney have any value at all, it is that they were taken as it happened, in the wild, and not contrived or manipulated. It was especially rewarding, therefore, when they were selected and formed the basis for the design of the Irish one pound coin, which carries the image of a native Killarney red deer stag.

There are other, less publicised but really worthwhile uses to be obtained from photographs of wild deer. One typical use in the case of the Killarney mountain herd of red deer is that of distinguishing male from female yearlings. There were times when I confidently noted down the sighting at dusk of a yearling female, only to find, when the transparency was enlarged by projection, the tell-tale evidence of two tiny nobs on the animal's forehead, the first signs of pedicle growth on a young male. Other obvious advantages are the recording of deer in the mountain habitat that had been tagged in the lowlands.

Finally, there were times in the mountains when, having stalked into the deer, I have hesitated and then held back from taking the photograph and instead put away the camera and just watched and savoured the scenes of wild deer life about me. To have pressed the shutter release would have broken the spell; for after all, no photograph can match the actual experiencing of wild nature. The best images are taken with our minds and stored in our memories.

Important Warning

It is again stressed that wild red stags cannot be trusted, especially during the rutting period. And the mountain environment is a harsh and unforgiving one; swift weather changes are normal, and can cause fatalities. The Kerry mountains are regularly underestimated and underrated. Since 1966, 35 people have been killed in them. Persons intending to venture into these mountains should be aware of the dangers inherent in all mountain terrain, and should seek advice from recognised mountaineering organisations.

V
Counting the Wild Red Deer

Commencing in 1970, yearly summer counts have been made of the mountain herd of red deer, with the exception of 1975, 1977 and 1984. The counters – the wildlife staff of Killarney National Park and experienced helpers – walk in line, about 200 to 300 hundred metres apart, and remain in speaking communication with each other throughout on walkie-talkies, and also maintain visual contact with each other. The areas covered are from the western boundary of the park at the Loughnambreacdearg and Coumeenslaun Lakes, moving eastwards over the Knockrower and Poulagower Hills, and then on over the Stompacoumeen and Dromderlough Hills; then descending through Coumeenaglasattin and Coumeen to cross the Crinneagh stream; and then over the Cores and Ferta moorland slopes to the eastern boundary at Failacurrane. Those on the highest part of the line keep to the high ground, along the top ridge of Dromderlough to Mangerton, counting deer on these higher slopes and meeting up with the other counters at Failacurrane. The count usually takes from six to eight hours. Deer run ahead of the line at first, then double back and easily break through the spaces in the line, being counted by each person only as they pass on his or her left. Total numbers of males, females and calves are recorded, as well as the time of counting – important in the event that deer may run uphill and be double counted. The separate hills of Cromagloun and Torc are normally counted by other persons on the same day, or else on the preceding or subsequent day. The areas of Toamies, Glena and Glasheennamarbh, which are separated from the main mountain habitat range of Mangerton and Torc by the Killarney Valley, are counted separately.

The results of yearly summer counts are set out in Table 3. From a total of 110 in 1970, the numbers increased to a high of 614 in 1991, and have since shown a trend of decline. This suggests that the total summer numbers of red deer in the mountains of Killarney National Park may have reached a peak of carrying capacity and have begun to even out. That carrying capacity is influenced by the presence of about 500 sika deer throughout the park, plus an estimated 2,000 unauthorised sheep that graze on the park mountain habitats, and plus approximately 100 feral goats that occupy mostly the steeper cliffs of Torc, but who also graze the mountain slopes.

Winter counts of the mountain herd of the Killarney red deer commenced in 1981. These are set out in Table 4. While the numbers reached a peak in 1992, the trend is a return to numbers more in line with the early 1980s.

Table 3. Deer Totals in Killarney – Summer

Year	Month	Stags	Hinds+Y	Calves	Total+a	Unidentified	Total+b
1970	July	25	60	25	110	N/A	110
1971	July	38	69	25	132	N/A	132
1972	July	45	78	32	155	N/A	155
1973	July	58	90	32	180	N/A	180
1974	July	61	94	36	191	N/A	191
1975	No Count						
1976	August	85	148	34	267	N/A	267
1977	No Count						
1978	October	93	134	53	280	N/A	280
1979	June	46	132	45	223	N/A	223
1980	September	92	153	38	283	30	313
1981	August	105	220	69	394	N/A	394
1982	September	91	147	62	300	N/A	300
1983	August	136	218	68	422	N/A	422
1984	No Count						
1985	July	123	244	59	426	N/A	426
1986	September	127	218	71	416	N/A	416
1987	August	112	297	70	479	4	483
1988	September	111	246	63	420	9	429
1989	August	119	311	93	523	N/A	523
1990	September	131	296	100	527	N/A	527
1991	August	124	356	134	614	N/A	614
1992	July	115	365	95	575	N/A	575
1993	July	81	258	69	408	N/A	408
1994	August	130	272	88	490	N/A	490
1995	August	82	307	68	457	N/A	457
1996	August	90	253	84	427	N/A	427
1997	September	109	215	80	404	N/A	404

Table 4. Deer Totals in Killarney – Winter

Year	Month	Stags	Hinds+Y	Calves	Total+a	Unidentified	Total+b
1981	April	61	130	48	239	N/A	239
1982	April	52	135	37	224	22	246
1983	No Count						
1984	December	58	109	28	195	N/A	195
1985	No Count						
1986	No Count						
1987	March	53	162	61	276	N/A	276
1988	No Count						
1989	April	57	134	33	224	16	240
1990	March	56	117	43	216	N/A	216
1991	No Count						
1992	February	79	200	89	368	N/A	368
1993	April	77	185	69	331	15	346
1994	No Count						
1995	April	46	142	36	224	N/A	224
1996	No Count						
1997	April	43	184	54	281	N/A	281

Notes and References

Chapter 1

1. Gerard Murphy, *Early Irish Lyrics,* Oxford, 1962, pp. 158–59.
2. For a comprehensive treatment of the wolf in Ireland, see James Fairley, *An Irish Beast Book,* Blackstaff, Belfast, 1984, pp. 288–311.
3. Personal communication from Park Ranger Peter O'Toole, Killarney National Park, June, 1995.
4. T. Clinton, T.J. Hayden, J.M. Lynch and P.J. Murphy, 'A Case of Twin Foetuses in a Sika Hind (*Cervus nippon*) from County Wicklow, Ireland' in *Deer,* Vol. 8, No. 7, 1992, pp. 437–39.
5. Brid Nowlan, 'Fox Attacking Sika Deer Calf' in *Irish Naturalists' Journal,* Vol. 22, No. 11, 1988, p. 502.
6. Roderick O'Flaherty, *West or H-Iar Connaught, written A.D. 1684,* The Irish Archaeological Society, Dublin, 1846, p. 12.
7. Personal correspondence dated 15 December 1983, from Dr A.B. Bubenik, wildlife biologist, Ontario, Canada.
8. Victor H. Cahalane, *Mammals of North America,* Macmillan, New York, 1966, p. 20.
9. Charles Georges Leroy, *The Intelligence and Perfectibility of Animals From a Philosophic Point of View,* Chapman & Hall, London, 1870, p. 45.
10. Raymond E. Chaplin, *Deer,* Blandford, Poole, 1977, p. 177.
11. *Ibid.,* pp. 76–77; and also T.H. Clutton-Brock and S.D. Albon, *Red Deer in the Highlands,* Oxford, 1989, pp. 83–85.
12. D.P. Sleeman, 'Parasites of Deer in Ireland' in *Journal of Life Sciences,* Royal Dublin Society, 1983, pp. 203–10.
13. William O. Pruitt, Jr., *Behaviour of the Barren-Ground Caribou,* University of Alaska, 1960, pp. 13–15.

Chapter 2

1. Gerard Murphy, *Early Irish Lyrics,* Oxford, 1962, pp. 68–69.
2. Raymond E. Chaplin, *Deer,* Blandford, 1977, p. 100.
3. G. Kenneth Whitehead, *Deer and Their Management in the Deer Parks of Great Britain and Ireland,* Country Life, London, 1950, p. 327. Whitehead's statement was based on a reply to his questionnaire circular for his book; the basis for hummels in Killarney is hearsay.
4. T. Carruthers, P. O'Leary, and J.B. O'Connor, 'Sika Deer Hummel?' in *Deer,* Vol. 6, No. 4, 1984, p. 144.
5. T.H. Clutton-Brock, F.E. Guinness and S.D. Albon, *Red Deer: Behaviour and Ecology of Two Sexes,* Edinburgh, 1982, p. 270; and T.H. Clutton-Brock and S.D. Albon, *Red Deer in the Highlands,* Oxford, 1989, pp. 123–25.

6. Rory Putman, *The Natural History of Deer*, Christopher Helm, London, 1988, pp. 151–52.
7. Allan Gordon Cameron, *The Wild Red Deer of Scotland*, Anthony Atha, Norfolk, (reprint 1984), p. 81.
8. Raymond E. Chaplin, *Deer*, Blandford, 1977, p. 103.

Chapter 3

1. Gerard Murphy, *Early Irish Lyrics*, Oxford, 1962, pp. 68–69.
2. Rory Putman, *The Natural History of Deer*, Christopher Helm, London, 1988, pp. 80–81.
3. *Ibid.*, p. 97.
4. For detailed descriptions and assessments of roaring, see T.H. Clutton-Brock, F.E. Guinness, and S.D. Albon, *Red Deer: Behaviour and Ecology of Two Species*, Edinburgh, 1982, pp. 135–39; and rutting displays, see pp. 107–17.
5. For original research on stag fighting, see T.H. Clutton-Brock; S.D. Albon; R.M. Gibson; and F.E. Guinness, 'The Logical Stag: Adaptive Aspects of Fighting in Red Deer (*Cervus elaphus* L.)' in *Animal Behaviour*, No. 27, 1979, pp. 211–25.
6. L.M. Nolan in 'News From Ireland', in *Deer*, Vol. 5, No. 9, 1982, p. 461.
7. As in 4 above, pp. 211–25.
8. T.H. Clutton-Brock and S.D. Albon, *Red Deer in the Highlands*, BSF Professional Books, Oxford, 1989, p. 51.
9. Karen McComb, 'Roaring by Red Stags Advances the Date of Oestrous in Hinds', in *Nature*, Letters [. . .] Vol. 330, 17 December 1987.
10. Clutton-Brock et al., *Red Deer in the Highlands*, p. 53.
11. *Ibid.*, p. 50.
12. R.M. Gibson and F.E. Guinness, 'Differential Reproduction Among Red Deer (*Cervus elaphus*) Stags on Rhum' in *Journal of Animal Ecology*, No. 49, 1980, pp. 199–208.
13. Clutton-Brock et al., *Red Deer in the Highlands*, pp. 50–51.
14. *Ibid.*, p. 54.

Chapter 4

1. Gerard Murphy, *Early Irish Lyrics*, Oxford, 1962, pp. 154–55.
2. P.K. Rohan, *The Climate of Ireland*, Stationery Office, Dublin, 1975, pp. 100–01.
3. J.R. Brindley, 'The Dispersion of the Lowland Red Deer Herd in the Killarney Valley, County Kerry, and Factors Contributing to it', in *Transactions of the International Congress of Game Biology*, No. 14, 1982, pp. 573–81.
4. Brian Mitchell, Brian W. Staines and David Welch, *Ecology of Red Deer*, Institute of Terrestrial Ecology, Banchory, 1977, p. 21.
5. *Ibid.*, p. 21.
6. 'Winter Kills 70,000 Beara Ewes', *The Cork Examiner*, 4 September 1986.
7. J.G. Millais, *The Mammals of Great Britain and Ireland*, Longmans, Green & Co, London, 1906, Vol. III, p. 124.

Chapter 5

1. Based on James Carney, *Medieval Irish Lyrics*, The Dolmen Press, Dublin, 1967, pp. 22–23; also in Kuno Meyer, *Selections from Ancient Irish Poetry*, Constable & Co., London, 1913, p. 57: author's part translation.
2. T.H. Clutton-Brock and S.D. Albon, *Red Deer in the Highlands*, Oxford, 1989, pp. 149–53.
3. Brian Mitchell, Brian W. Staines and David Welch, *Ecology of Red Deer*, Institute of Terrestrial Ecology, Banchory, 1977, pp. 16–17.

4. R.R. Hofmann, 'Morphological Classification of Sika Deer Within the Comparative System of Ruminant Feeding Types', in *Deer*, Vol. 5, No. 7, 1982, pp. 352–53.
5. Richard J. Goss, *Deer Antlers: Regeneration, Function, and Evolution*, Academic Press, New York, 1983, pp. 141–48.

Chapter 6

1. Gerard Murphy, *Early Irish Lyrics*, Oxford, 1962, pp. 164–65.
2. John Riney, *The Red Deer of County Kerry*, unpublished confidential report to the Parks Division, Office of Public Works, 1974, pp. 9–12.
3. Brian Vesey-Fitzgerald, *British Game*, New naturalist, Collins, London, 1946, p. 186.
4. T.H. Clutton-Brock, F.E. Guinness and S.D. Albon, *Red Deer: Behaviour and Ecology of Two Sexes*, Edinburgh University Press, 1982, pp. 84–98.
5. B. Mitchell, D. McCowan and I.A. Nicholson, 'Annual Cycles of Body Weight and Condition in Scottish Red Deer, *Cervus elaphus*', in *Journal of Zoology*, London, 1976, No. 180, pp. 107–27.

Appendix 2

1. *Cork Examiner*, 4 September 1986. The article 'Winter Kills 70,000 Beara Ewes' detailed sheep losses in the Beara Peninsula of West Cork during the winter of 1985–86.
2. *The Kerryman*, 4 January 1991. The article 'Call for Action After Deer Death' detailed the drowning of a red deer in an artificial pool in Killarney Golf Course.
3. Brid Nowlan, 'Fox Attacking Sika Deer Calf' in *Irish Naturalists' Journal*, Vol. 22, No. 11, 1988, p. 502.
4. D.P. Sleeman and J.S. Gray, 'Some Observations on Fly-Worry of Deer' in *Mammal Society Notes*, No. 45, 1982, pp. 535–41; D.P. Sleeman, 'Parasites of Deer in Ireland', in *Journal of Life Sciences*, RDS, 1983, pp. 203–10.
5. D.P. Sleeman, 'Larvae of *Cephenomyia auribarbis* (Meigen) and *Hypoderma diana* (Diptera: Oestridae) from a Red Deer, *Cervus elaphus* L., in County Donegal, in *Irish Naturalists' Journal*, Vol. 19, No. 12, 1979, pp. 441–42.
6. T.G. Palferman, 'Lyme Disease: an Overview' in *Deer*, Vol. 8, No. 9, 1992, pp. 567–69.
7. E.A. Collen, 'News from Ireland' (detailing the negative results of tests for Lyme disease on 60 Irish deer: 30 in County Cork and 30 in County Wicklow) in *Deer*, Vol. 7, No. 8, 1989, p. 429.
8. P.L. Davenport, 'Risks for Stalkers in Ireland' (T.B. in Wicklow Deer) in *Deer*, Vol. 6, No. 9, 1986, p. 381.
9. Matt Hyland, 'News From Ireland' (detailing levels of T.B. recorded in Ireland: '. . . of the 1,000 sika culled in the National Park, Killarney, only one was infected with T.B. About 3% of T.B. infection is the general level recorded for free living sika deer in Wicklow, and in the recent tests on the Phoenix Park fallow deer infection was in the region of 4%') in *Deer*, Vol. 8, No. 8, 1992, p. 536.

Appendix 3

1. G.R. Iason, C.D. Duck and T.H. Clutton-Brock, 'Grazing and Reproductive Success of Red Deer: the Effects of Local Enrichment by Gull Colonies' in *Journal of Animal Ecology*, No. 55, 1986, pp. 507–15.
2. Michael Brooke, *The Manx Shearwater*, T. and A.D. Poyser, London, 1990, pp. 49–50; and report by P. Wormell, 'Red Deer (*Cervus elaphus*) as Predator on Manx Shearwater (*Procellaria puffinus*), in *Deer*, Vol. 1, No. 8, 1969, p. 289.
3. Ageing by tooth analysis of the Inishvicillaun red hind jawbone by Fiona Lang and John Long, Dept. of Zoology, University College, Dublin, June 1991.

Bibliography

Select Bibliography of works on deer biology, and of recent literature relevant to the Killarney red and sika deer, and to Irish deer in general. Historical works, and historical references to Irish deer, are not included.

The publication *Deer* is the Journal of the British Deer Society.

Albon, S.D. and Iarson, G.R., 'Control of Fertility in Red Deer' in *Nature* Vol. 307, 1984.

Albon, S.D., Staines, H.J., Guinness, F.E. and Clutton-Brock, T.H., 'Density-dependent Changes in the Spacing Behaviour of Female Kin in Red Deer' in *Journal of Animal Ecology* 1992.

Blaxter, K.L., Kay, R.N.B. and Sharman, G.A.M., *Farming the Red Deer.* HMSO, 1974.

Brindley, J.B., *Ecology and Population Dynamics of the Lowland Red Deer Herd in Killarney, County Kerry, Ireland.* M.Sc. Thesis, unpublished, University College, Dublin, 1980.

Brindley, J.R., 'The Dispersion of the Lowland Red Deer Herd in the Killarney Valley, County Kerry and Factors Contributing to it' in *Transactions of the International Congress of Game Biology*, No. 14, 1982.

Burkitt, T.D., 'Sika Deer Management in Killarney National Park' in *Deer* Vol. 9, No. 2, 1993.

Cameron, A.G., *The Wild Red Deer of Scotland.* 1923. Anthony Atha, Norfolk (reprint), 1984.

Canny, M., 'Deer and the Republic of Ireland Wildlife Service' in *Deer* Vol. 8, No. 4, 1991.

Carne, P., 'Kerry Deer Day' in *Shooting Times & Country Magazine* May 1974.

Carne, P.H., 'The Distribution of Wild and Feral Deer in Great Britain and Ireland' in *Deer* Vol. 5, No. 7, 1982.

Carruthers, T., O'Leary, P. and O'Connor, J.B., 'Sika Deer Hummel [in Killarney]?' in *Deer* Vol. 6, No. 4, 1984.

Chaplin, R.E., *Deer.* Blandford Press, Poole, 1977.

Chapman, N., *Deer.* Whittet Books, London, 1991.

Clinton, T., Hayden, T.J., Lynch, J.M. and Murphy, P., 'A Case of Twin Foetuses in a Sika Hind (*Cervus nippon*) from County Wicklow, Ireland' in *Deer* Vol. 8, No. 7, 1992.

Clutton-Brock, T.H., Albon, S.D., Gibson, R.M. and Guinness, F.E., 'The Logical Stag: Adaptive Aspects of Fighting in Red Deer (*Cervus elaphus L.*)' in *Animal Behaviour*, Vol. 27, 1979.

Clutton-Brock, T.H., Guinness, F.E. and Albon, S.D., 'The Costs of Reproduction to Red Deer Hinds' in *Journal of Animal Ecology*, Vol. 52, 1983.

Clutton-Brock, T.H., 'Reproductive Success in Red Deer' in *Scientific American*, Vol. 252, No. 2, February 1985.

Clutton-Brock, T.H., Guinness, F.E. and Albon, S.D., *Red Deer: Behaviour and Ecology of Two Sexes.* Edinburgh University Press, 1982.

Clutton-Brock, T. H. and Albon, S.D., *Red Deer in the Highlands.* BSP Professional Books, Oxford, 1989.

Clutton-Brock, T.H., 'Red Deer and Man' in *National Geographic* Vol. 170, No. 4, 1986.

Clutton-Brock, T.H. and Albon, S.D., 'The Accuracy of Red Deer Counts' in *Deer*, Vol. 8, No. 1, 1990.

Clutton-Brock, T.H. and Albon, S.D., 'Trial and Error in the Highlands' in *Nature*, Vol. 358, July 1992.

Collen, E.A., 'News from Ireland' (Lyme disease – negative test results from 60 Irish deer) in *Deer*, Vol. 7, No. 8, 1989.

Cork Examiner, 9 June 1967. 'Killarney Valley as a Special Amenity Area?' (reported statements by the Parliamentary Secretary to the Minister for Finance: the red deer must be preserved, and it was decided to discontinue sheep farming in the park).

Cork Examiner, 29 February 1980. 'Charlie's Four Bambies' (OPW confirmed that four red deer from Killarney were to be transferred to Inisvickillaun, where there would be no danger of cross-breeding with sika deer, and thus preserve the purity of the herd).

Cork Examiner, 31 January 1984. 'Killarney Park to Cease as Forestry' (Government decision that continuing afforestation in Killarney National Park was incompatible with National Park policies).

Cork Examiner, 21 May 1986. 'Butcher Fined Under Wildlife Act' (conviction for keeping a sika carcase for sale).

Cork Examiner, 4 September 1986. 'Winter Kills 70,000 Beara Ewes' (sheep losses in the Beara Penninsula during winter of 1985–86).

Cork Examiner, 11 October 1990. 'Killarney Deer Under Threat' (competition for grazing from sika deer and trespassing sheep).

Cork Examiner, 1 April 1991. 'Deer Plan Rejected' (request to introduce sika deer to the West of Ireland refused, as it was not the policy of the Wildlife Service to introduce wild deer into new areas).

Cork Examiner, 22 April 1993. 'Warning to Farmers after Goring Death' (extreme caution urged after man gored to death by a red stag on a deer farm).

Cork Examiner, 15 June 1993. 'Need to Conserve Sika Deer in Killarney' (reported Dr Rory Harrington of the National Parks and Wildlife Service stating at an international symposium in Killarney that the introduced Japanese sika deer in Killarney were just as worthy of conservation as the native red deer).

Craig, A.J., *Killarney National Park, an Introductory Guide*. O.P.W., Dublin, 1983.

Craig, A.J., 'National Parks and Other Conservation Areas' in *Nature Conservation in Ireland: Progress and Problems*. Jeffrey, D.W. ed., Royal Irish Academy, Dublin, 1984.

Cronin, P., 'News from Ireland' (Number and expansion of sika deer in Kerry) in *Deer*, Vol. 4, No. 5, 1978.

Cummins, J., 'Red Deer in Ireland' (Past and present numbers) in *Deer*, Vol. 4, No. 6, 1978.

Dansie, O., 'Live-Catching Sika Deer at Killarney, South-West Ireland' in *Deer*, Vol. 4, 1979.

Dansie, O., 'The Case for Catching Deer – Part III' in *Deer*, Vol. 9, No. 2, 1993.

Darling, F. Fraser, *A Herd of Red Deer*. Oxford University Press, London, 1937.

Davenport, P.L., (transl.): 'Risk for Stalkers in Ireland' (T.B. in Wicklow deer) in *Deer*, Vol. 6, No. 9, 1986.

Deane, C.D., 'Deer in Ireland' in *Deer*, Vol. 2, No. 9, 1972.

Delap, P., 'Deer in Wicklow' in *The Irish Naturalists' Journal*, Vol. VI, No. 4, 1936.

Delap, P., 'Some Notes on the Social Habits of the British Deer' in *Proceedings of the Zoological Society*, London, 1957.

deNahlik, A.J., *Deer Management*. David & Charles, London, 1974.

deNahlik, A.J., *Wild Deer: Culling, Conservation and Management*. Ashford Press Publishing, Southampton, 1987.

Fairley, J.S., 'New Records of Deer in Ireland' in *The Irish Naturalists' Journal*, Vol. XVI, 1970, and Supplement to same, also Vol. XVI, 1970.

Fairley, J.S., *An Irish Beast Book*. The Blackstaff Press, Belfast, 1984.

Fairley, J.S., *Irish Wild Mammals: a Guide to the Literature*. Privately published, Galway, 1992.

Foras Forbartha, An. *Areas of Scientific Interest in Ireland*. Dublin, 1981.

Gibson, R.M. and Guinness, F.E., 'Differential Reproduction Among Red Deer (*Cervus elaphus*) Stags on Rhum' in *Journal of Animal Ecology*, No. 49, 1980.

Gordon, I.J., 'Facilitation of Red Deer Grazing by Cattle and its Impact on Red Deer Performance' in *Journal of Applied Ecology*, Vol. 25, 1988.

Goss, R.J., *Deer Antlers; Regeneration, Function and Evolution*. Academic Press, New York, 1983.

Grace, J. and Easterbee, N., 'The Natural Shelter for Red Deer (*Cervus elaphus*) in a Scottish Glen' in *Journal of Applied Ecology*, Vol. 16, 1979.

Guinness, F.E., Clutton-Brock, T.H. and Albon, S.D., 'Factors Affecting Calf Mortality in Red Deer (*Cervus elaphus*)' in *Journal of Animal Ecology*, Vol. 47, 1978.

Guinness, F. E., Hall, M.J. and Cockerill, R.A., 'Mother-Offspring Association in Red Deer (*Cervus elaphus L.*) on Rhum' in *Animal Behaviour*, Vol. 27, 1979.

Habicht, G.S., Beck, G. and Benach, J.L., 'Lyme Disease' in *Scientific American*, Vol. 257, No. 1, July, 1987.

Harrington, R., 'Hybridisation Among Deer and its Implications for Conservation' in *Irish Forestry*, Vol. 30, 1973.

Harrington, R., 'The Hybridisation of Red Deer and Sika Deer in Northern Ireland' in *Irish Forestry*, Vol. 31, 1974.

Harrington, R., 'Exotic Deer in Ireland' in *The Introduction of Exotic Species: Advantages and Problems*, Royal Irish Academy, Dublin, 1979.

Harrington, R., 'The Hybridisation of Red Deer (*Cervus elaphus L.* 1758) and Japanese Sika Deer (*C. nippon* Temminck 1838)' in *Transactions of the International Congress of Game Biology*, No. 14, 1982.

Harrington, R., 'Evolution and Distribution of the Cervidae' in *The Royal Society of New Zealand*, Bulletin 22, 1985.

Harrington, R., 'Aspects of Hybridisation, Immuno–Taxonomy and Kartotypes within the Genus Cervus' in *1st Symposium on Genetics of Wild Animals,* Giessen, 1985.

Harris, R.A. and Duff, K.R., *Wid Deer in Britain.* Newton Abbot, 1970

Hayden, T.J., Moore, N.A. and Kelly, P.F. 'The Fallow Deer of Phoenix Park: An Evolving Management Plan' in *Management, Welfare and Conservation of Park Deer,* Bullock, D.J. and Goldspink, C.R. eds., Universities Federation for Animal Welfare, 1992.

Hofmann, R.R., 'Morphological Classification of Sika Deer within the Comparative System of Ruminant Feeding Types' in *Deer,* Vol. 5, No. 7, 1982.

Hyland, M., 'News from Ireland' (Killarney red deer in Doneraile Forest Park) in *Deer,* Vol. 8, No. 2, 1990.

Hyland, M., 'News from Ireland' (deer poaching in Wicklow) in *Deer,* Vol. 8, No. 7, 1992.

Hyland, M., 'News from Ireland' (T.B. recorded in Irish deer) in *Deer,* Vol. 8, No. 8, 1992.

Iason, G.R., Duck, C.D. and Clutton-Brock, T.H., 'Grazing and Reproductive Success of Red Deer: the Effect of Local Enrichment by Gull Colonies' in *Journal of Animal Ecology,* No. 55, 1986.

Irish Times, 11 November 1963. 'Red Deer Fewer at Killarney'.

Irish Times, 17 December, 1971. 'What's to be Done About Killarney?'

Irish Times, 19 December, 1973. 'Taking Care of the Deer Population'.

Irish Times, 18 September 1984. 'A Future for Deer Farming' (reported Rory Harrington, Department of Wildlife, outlining the advantages of hybrid deer for deer farming).

Kerryman, 16 November 1963. 'Killarney's Red Deer are not Disappearing'.

Kerryman, 20 November 1981. Wildlife Wardens, Killarney National Park, Letter to the Editor – Shooting Deer (pointing out that Councillor Jackie Healy-Rae's suggestion that deer in Kerry 'should be shot on sight' was contrary to the provisions of the Wildlife Act, 1976).

Kerryman, 4 January 1991. 'Call for Action After Deer Death' (red deer drowned in artificial pond in Killarney Golf Course).

Kingdom, 25 January 1994. 'Killarney's Red Deer Under Threat' (concern at transfer by OPW of 16 hybrid deer to Doneraile Park, 30 miles from Killarney).

Kilpatrick, C., 'Deer in Ulster – I' in *Deer,* Vol. 6, No. 9, 1986.

Kilpatrick, C., 'Deer in Ulster – II' in *Deer,* Vol. 6, No. 10, 1986.

Kilpatrick, C., 'Deer in Ulster – III' in *Deer,* Vol. 7, No. 1, 1986.

Kilpatrick, C., 'Deer in Ulster – IV' in *Deer,* Vol. 7, No. 2, 1987.

Larner, J.B., *An Irish Herd of Sika Deer.* M.Sc. Thesis, University College, Dublin, 1972.

Larner, J.B., 'Sika Deer Damage to Mature Woodlands of South-western Ireland' in *Proceedings of the International Congress of Game Biology,* No. 13, 1977.

Larner, J.B., *The Impact of a Herd of Sika Deer on their Woodland Habitat.* Ph.D. Thesis, University College, Dublin, 1980.

Larner, J.B., 'The Feeding Range Size of Sika Deer in South-west Ireland' in *Transactions of the International Congress of Game Biology,* No. 14, 1982.

Leroy, C.G., *The Intelligence and Perfectibility of Animals From a Philosophic Point of View.* Chapman & Hall, London, 1870.

Lewin, R., 'Rutting on Rhum' in *New Scientist,* Vol. 80, No. 1129, November, 1978.

Lincoln, G.A., 'Biology of Antlers' in *Journal of Zoology,* Vol. 226, Part 3, 1992.

Linnell, J.D.C., *The Biochemical Systematics of Red and Sika Deer in Ireland.* B.Sc.(Hons.) Thesis, University College, Cork, 1989.

Long, P., 'Killarney's Native Reds – The Situation in '84' in *Field and Countryside,* Vol. 2 No. 3, 1985.

Lowe, V.P.W., 'Teeth as Indicators of Age With Special Reference to Red Deer (*Cervus elaphus L.*) of Known Age From Rhum' in *Journal of Zoology,* Vol. 152, London, 1967.

Lowe, V.P.W., 'Population Dynamics of the Red Deer (*Cervus elaphus L.*) on Rhum' in *Journal of Animal Ecology,* No. 38, 1969.

Lowe, V.P.W. and Gardiner, A.S., 'A Re-examination of the Subspicies of Red Deer (*Cervus elaphus*) With Particular Reference to the Stocks in Britain' in *Journal of Zoology,* London, Vol. 174, 1974.

Lowe, V.P.W. and Gardiner, A.S., 'Hybridisation between Red deer (*Cervus elaphus*) and Sika deer (*Cervus nippon*) with particular reference to stocks in N.W. England' in *Journal of Zoology,* London, Vol. 177, 1975.

Lynch, J.M. and Hayden, T.J., 'Use of Multivariate Techniques to Separate Cervid Populations in Ireland' in *Proceedings of the Third Irish Zoologists Meeting,* University College, Dublin, 1989.

Lynch, J.M., *Aspects of Growth and Morphology of Japanese Sika Deer from Killarney National Park.* B.Sc. Thesis, University College, Dublin, 1989.

Lynch, J.M., O'Corry-Crowe, G. and Hayden, T.J., 'Morphology of the Antlers of the Sika Deer, *Cervus nippon,* from the Killarney Valley' in *Mammal Society Conference,* 1989.

Mac Lochlainn, C.P., *Aspects of the Ecology of Red Deer in Glenveigh National Park, County Donegal*. M.Sc. Thesis, University College, Dublin, 1982.

MacLochlainn, C., 'The Kerry Deer Society' in *Field and Streem*, Vol. 2, No. 8, 1985.

MacNally, L., *Highland Year*. Phoenix Press, London, 1968.

MacNally, L., *The Year of the Red Deer*. J.M.Dent & Sons Ltd., London, 1975.

MacNally, L., *Highland Deer Forest*. Pan Books Ltd., London, 1970.

MacNally, L., 'Starving to Death' (widespread winter mortality in Scottish red deer) in *Shooting Times*, June, 1989.

McCabe, R.A., 'Management Recommendations for Native Irish Red Deer' in *XV Congr. Int. Fauna Cinegetica y Silvestre*, 1983.

McComb, K., 'Roaring by Red Stags Advances the Date of Oestros in Hinds' in *Nature*, Vol. 330, 1987.

McCurdy, J., 'Sika Deer in Ireland: A Success Story' in *Deer*, Vol. 7, No. 5, 1988.

McCurdy, R.J., 'Deer Management in Northern Ireland' in *Deer*, Vol. 8, No. 4, 1991.

McDiarmid, A., 'Enzootic Ataxia of Deer' in *Deer*, Vol. 2, No. 8, 1972.

McGarry, L., 'News from Ireland' (hybridisation of red and sika deer in County Wicklow) in *Deer*, Vol. 2, No. 10, 1973.

McGarry, L., 'News from Ireland' (hybrid deer in Wicklow – 'no red deer remaining there' – according to R. Harrington) in *Deer*, Vol. 3, No. 1, 1973.

McGarry, L., 'News from the Irish Deer Society' (Death of Miss Grace Drennan in the Killarney mountains, while on excursion to see the red deer) in *Deer*, Vol. 3, No. 5, 1974.

McQuiston, I.B., 'Protection for Ulster's Deer' in *Deer*, Vol. 6, No. 7, 1985.

Millais, J.G., *British Deer and Their Horns*. Henry Sothern & Co., London, 1897.

Mitchell, B., McCowan, D. and Nicholson, I.A., 'Annual Cycles of Body Weight and Condition in Scottish Red Deer, *Cervis elaphus*' in *Journal of Zoology*, Vol. 180, London, 1976.

Mitchell, B., Staines, B.W. and Welch, D., *Ecology of Red Deer*. Institute of Terrestrial Ecology, Banchory, 1977.

Moffat, C.B., *The Mammals of Ireland*. Proceedings of the Royal Irish Academy, Vol. XLIV, Section B, No. 6, 1938.

Mooney, O.V., 'Irish Deer and Forest Relations' in *Irish Forestry*, Vol. IX, No. 1, 1952.

Morrissey, A.A., 'Notes from the Irish Deer Society' (Numbers of red deer in Ireland), in *Deer*, Vol. 1, No. 7, 1968.

Morrissey, A.A., 'Deer and the Poacher in Ireland' in *Deer*, Vol. 2, No. 3, 1970.

Mulloy, F., 'A Note on the Occurrence of Deer in Ireland' in *Deer*, Vol. 2, No. 2, 1970.

Mulloy, F., 'Ireland's Deer' in *Ireland of the Welcomes*, Vol. 23, No. 8, 1974.

Murphy, P., Bolger, T. and Hayden T.J., 'The Morphology of the Skull of the Sika Deer, *Cervus nippon nippon*, from Wicklow and Killarney, and Red Deer, *Cervus elaphus*, from Donegal' in *Ungulate Research Group Conference*, 1988.

Nolan, L.M., 'News from Ireland' (two red/sika hybrid skeletons with interlocked antlers) in *Deer*, Vol. 5, No. 9, 1982.

Nolan, L.M., 'News from Ireland' (tag system introduced for deer shot on State land) in *Deer*, Vol. 6, No. 3, 1984.

Nolan, L., 'Irish Deer Society Policies and Recommendations' in *Deer*, Vol. 8, No. 4, 1991.

Nowlan, B., 'Fox Attacking Sika Deer Calf' in *Irish Naturalists' Journal*, Vol. 22, No. 11, 1988.

Nowlan B., *Niche Overlap of Three Herbivorous Species in Killarney National Park*. M.Ag.Sc. Thesis, University College, Dublin, 1989.

Nowlan, B., *The Population Dynamics of the Red Deer Herd in Killarney National Park, County Kerry, Ireland*. Report to the Office of Public Works, unpublished, 1990.

Nowlan, B. and O'Toole, P., *A Preliminary Survey of the Lowland Herd of Red Deer (Cervus elaphus) in Killarney National Park, County Kerry, Ireland*. Unpublished report to the Office of Public Works, 1991.

O'Corry-Crowe, G., *Morphology of the Skull and Antlers of Sika Deer from the Killarney Valley*. B.Sc. Thesis, University College, Dublin, 1988.

O'Donoghue, A. and Hayden, T., 'The Reproductive Biology of the Japanese Sika Deer, *Cervus nippon nippon*, From Killarney National Park' in *Proceedings of the Third Irish Zoologists' Meeting*, University College, Dublin, 1989.

O'Donoghue, Y.A., *Aspects of Growth and Reproduction of Japanese Sika Deer from Killarney National Park*. B.Sc. Thesis, University College, Dublin, 1986.

O'Donoghue, Y.A., *Growth, Reproduction and Survival in a Feral Population of Japanese Sika Deer*. Ph. D. Thesis, University College, Dublin, 1991.

Office of Public Works. *Killarney National Park Management Plan*. Stationery Office, Dublin, 1990.

O'Gorman, F., 'A Note on the Status of Deer at Killarney, County Kerry and a Programme for Research into their Management and Conservation' in *Deer News*, Vol. 1, No. 8, 1965.

O'Gorman, F., 'Irish Deer as a Valuable Natural Resource' in *National Game Council Report*, 1965.

O'Gorman, F., 'Some Aspects of Deer Ecology in Killarney, County Kerry' in *Bulletin of the Mammal Society of the British Isles,* Vol. 28, 1967.

O'Gorman, F. and Mulloy, F., 'The Economical and Recreational Potential of Deer in Ireland' in *The Future of Irish Wildlife – A Blueprint for Development,* O'Gorman, F. and Wymes, E., eds., Department of Lands & An Foras Taluntais, Dublin, 1973.

Osborne, B.C., 'Habitat use by Red Deer (*Cervus elaphus L.*) and Hill Sheep in the West Highlands' in *Journal of Applied Ecology,* Vol. 21, 1984.

O'Sullivan, E., *The Irish Deer Farming Industry – A Positive Outlook?* B.B.S. Thesis, University of Limerick, 1993.

O'Toole P. and Long, A., *A Study of the Distribution of the Lowland Red Deer Population in Killarney National Park.* Unpublished report to the OPW, January 1993.

O'Toole, P. and Long, A., *Update on the Distribution of the Lowland Red Deer Population in Killarney National Park.* Unpublished report to the OPW, August, 1993.

O'Toole, P. and Long, A., *The 1994 Update on the Distribution of the Lowland Red Deer Population in Killarney National Park.* Unpublished report ot the OPW, June, 1994.

O'Toole, P. and Ryan, S., *Natural Mortality in the Mountain Herd of Native Irish Red Deer in Killarney National Park during the Winters of 1993–94 and 1994–95.* Unpublished report to the NPWS, November, 1995.

Place, J.W., 'News from Ireland' (proposed cull of 750 sika in Killarney) in *Deer,* Vol. 4, No. 2, 1977.

Place, J.W., 'News from Ireland' (use of nets to capture deer in Killarney – for and against) in *Deer,* Vol. 4, No. 8, 1979.

Place, J.W., 'The Development of Deer Farming in Ireland' (concern on velvet harvesting) in *Deer,* Vol. 7, No. 5, 1988.

Putman, R., *The Natural History of Deer.* Christopher Helm, London, 1988.

Putman, R., 'Flexibility of Social Organisation and Reproductive Strategy in Deer' in *Deer,* Vol. 9, No. 1, 1993.

Putman, R.J. and Hunt, E.J., 'Hybridisation Between Red and Sika Deer in Britain' in *Deer,* Vol. 9, No. 2, 1993.

Quirke, C., *The Diet of Red Deer, Sika Deer and Scottish Blackface Sheep in Killarney National Park.* M.Sc. Thesis, University College, Dublin, 1991.

Ratcliffe, P.R., 'Distribution and Current Status of Sika Deer, *Cervus nippon,* in Great Britain' in *Mammal Review,* Vol. 17, No. 1, 1987.

Riney, J., *The Red Deer of County Kerry.* Unpublished confidential report to the OPW, 1974.

Rod & Gun, Vol. 3, No 2, 1980 ; 'Kilarney Red Deer for Blasket Island'.

Ryan, C.P., 'News from Ireland' (sale and export of 42 sika deer from Killarney to Dubai) in *Deer,* Vol. 4, No. 3, 1977.

Sherlock, M.G. and Fairley, J.S., 'Seasonal Changes in the Diet of Red Deer *Cervus elaphus* in the Connemara National Park' in *Proceedings of the Royal Irish Academy,* Vol. 93B, No. 2, 1993.

Sleeman, D.P., 'Larvae of *Cephenomyia auribarbis* (Meigen) and *Hypoderma diana* Baur (Diptera:Oestridae) From a Red Deer, *Cervus elaphus* L., in County Donegal' in *Irish Naturalists' Journal,* Vol. 19, No. 12, 1979.

Sleeman, D.P. and Gray, J.S., 'Some Observations on Fly-Worry of Deer' in *Mammal Society Notes,* No. 45, 1982.

Sleeman, D.P., *Parasites of Deer in Ireland.* Journal of Life Sciences, RDS, 1983.

Staines, B.W., 'The Use of Natural Shelter by Red Deer (*Cervus elaphus*) in Relation to Weather in North-East Scotland' in *Journal of Zoology,* Vol. 180, London, 1976.

Staines, B.W., 'The Dynamics and Performance of a Declining Population of Red Deer (*Cervus elaphus*)' in *Journal of Zoology,* Vol. 184, London, 1978.

Sunday Press, 13 January 1974. 'The Deer Nobody Loves' (report that Mr Rory Harrington, Dept. of Lands, advised that Sika deer could endanger the native Killarney red deer through hybrid breeding).

Thouless, C.R. and Guinness, F.E., 'Conflict Between Red Deer Hinds: The Winner Always Wins' in *Animal Behaviour,* Vol. 34, 1986.

Warner, P., 'Practical Aspects of Deer Management and Conservation in Ireland' in *Deer,* Vol. 8, No. 4, 1991.

Wigan, M., *Stag at Bay: The Scottish Red Deer Crisis.* Swan-Hill Press, Shrewsbury, 1993.

Wormell, P., 'Red Deer (*Cervus elaphus*) as Predator on Manx Shearwater (*Procellaria puffinus*)' in *Deer,* Vol. 1, No. 8, 1969.

Index

Page numbers in italics indicate illustrations